Praise for *Journeys North, Journey's End*

"A straightforward, often wryly witty and self-deprecating, telling of Young's remarkable life of dedication to improving the health of Indigenous people in Canada. From his humble beginnings as the youngest of 10 children in Hong Kong to becoming Dean of Public Health at the University of Alberta, Young reflects on how his cross-cultural experiences on virtually every continent inspired and enriched his commitment to ending the health disparities endured by Indigenous communities in Canada."

—ANN HERRING, Professor Emerita,
Department of Anthropology, McMaster University, Canada

"In his book, Dr Kue Young takes the reader through his life and career in public health. Born and raised in Hong Kong, Kue Young became a pioneer of circumpolar health research. He has put his open and inquisitive mind to full use, and everything he has touched, from the health clinic in the Sioux Lookout Zone to a teaching post in Tanzania and back to the Canadian Arctic, has been turned into a fascinating narrative. One has always wondered where he got his strength from and this book gives the answer. From his childhood in Hong Kong via university studies in Canada, Kue Young's academic focus evolved into a compassion for the underprivileged peoples of Northern Canada, not as the treatment of individuals but as improvement of their living conditions."

—PETER BJERREGAARD, Professor of Arctic Health,
Centre for Public Health Research in Greenland,
University of Southern Denmark, Denmark

"Dr Kue Young's life story is a testament to humility, vision, and service. His mentorship and early support were instrumental in helping me establish the Qaujigiartiit Health Research Centre in Iqaluit—believing in the strength of local leadership in the North. This book is a moving testament to his life trajectory from Hong Kong to Canada to Indigenous and northern communities told through personal narratives, humour, and an unwavering commitment to public health."

OWEN HEALEY AKEAROK, Director,
Qaujigiartiit Health Research Centre, Iqaluit, Nunavut

"Dr Kue Young's memoir will likely be of interest and value to anyone interested in how curiosity, talent, hard work and drive combined to create a meaningful career in public health, global health and academic leadership. From descriptions of his hardscrabble childhood roots in Hong Kong through years of dedicated service in low-resource settings, completion of multiple degrees, selection to diverse leadership roles, extensive global travel and receipt of high national and international honours, this reflective book provides a front row seat to not only the trajectory of one remarkable life, but also many of the social forces that have transformed public health practice, health workforce pipelines, academic careers, and our understandings of what best promotes health and well-being around the globe and in the Arctic, particularly in Indigenous communities. Those fortunate to have known Dr Young at any stage of his long career may also gain additional insight into how and why he became the influential, driven, productive, humble Arctic public health leader and mentor that he has long been. Highly recommended."

—RHONDA M JOHNSON, Professor of Public Health,
University of Alaska Anchorage, USA

"This is a remarkable and inspirational journey of a doctor born and raised in Hong Kong, who went on to work for the health and wellbeing of Canada's Indigenous people, as practitioner, researcher, and administrator."

—CHANDRAKANT SHAH, Professor Emeritus,
Dalla Lana School of Public Health, University of Toronto, Canada

"What a pleasure it is to read Kue Young's memoir! His journey from Hong Kong to northern Canada, with periodic stops on other continents, is grounded in his sense of social justice, and his profound understanding that social inequality within societies has tremendous consequences on human health. To change the conditions he saw as a physician delivering health care in northern Indigenous settlements, he embarked on more formal learning and accepted administrative responsibilities to lead Departments and Schools of Public Health at major Canadian research universities. There, the formation of cross-culturally competent health care workers not only demands a two-way flow of ideas but also builds respect among Indigenous and non-Indigenous students and practitioners. His humour, sometimes self-directed, makes the reader laugh; the brief tales of his administrative experiences show a man who speaks his mind. His love of the north, especially its Indigenous peoples, echo deep in the reader's heart. Kue Young's memoir is worth reading by anyone who has ever asked, 'Why am I here?'"

—EMŐKE J E SZATHMÁRY, President Emeritus,
Professor Emeritus and Senior Scholar, University of Manitoba

Journeys North
Journey's End

KUE YOUNG

MAWENZI
HOUSE

We acknowledge the support of the Canada Council for the Arts for our publishing program. We also acknowledge support from the Government of Ontario through the Ontario Arts Council, and the support of the Government of Canada through the Canada Book Fund.

Cover design by Mei Linh Cheng

Library and Archives Canada Cataloguing in Publication

Title: Journeys north, journey's end / Kue Young.

Names: Young, T. Kue, author.

Identifiers: Canadiana (print) 20250214571 | Canadiana (ebook) 20250216663 | ISBN 9781774151952 (softcover) | ISBN 9781774151969 (EPUB) | ISBN 9781774151976 (PDF)

Subjects: LCSH: Young, T. Kue. | LCSH: Indigenous peoples—Medical care—Canada, Northern. | LCSH: Indigenous peoples—Health and hygiene—Canada, Northern. | LCSH: Rural health services—Canada, Northern. | LCSH: College teachers—Canada—Biography. | LCGFT: Autobiographies.

Classification: LCC RA450.4.I53 Y68 2025 | DDC 362.1089/970719—dc23

Printed and bound in Canada by Coach House Printing

Mawenzi House Publishers Ltd.
192 Spadina Ave, Suite 417
Toronto, ON, M5T 2C2
Canada

www.mawenzihouse.com

Contents

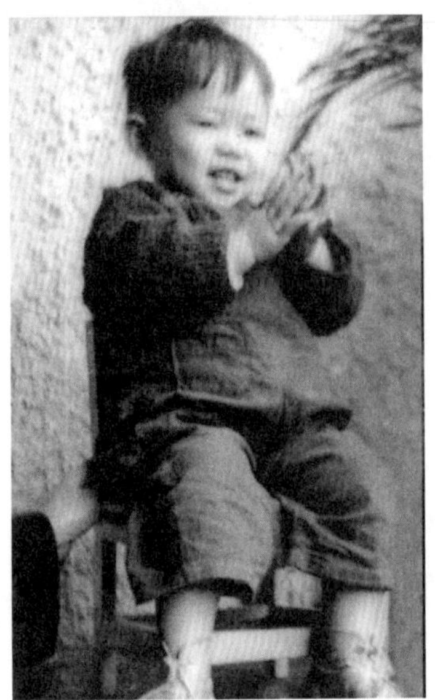

Journey's beginning, Hong Kong, circa 1950

1.

Pre-Text

People who write their memoirs owe the readers an explanation. Can they justify why they indulge in personal introspection and reflection at the end of their professional careers? Why should people other than friends, families, and former colleagues be interested in their innermost thoughts and opinions?

So, what is my "pretext"?

I arrived in Canada from Hong Kong in 1966 at the age of eighteen, to attend McGill University. Subsequently I devoted almost my entire professional academic career working with, among, and for northern and Indigenous communities in Canada and abroad. This book traces the personal journeys I have undertaken and provides the context and background to my rather unusual and winding career path. It is part memoir, part political and historical discussion, and a part primer on Northern, Indigenous, and Global Health. Although I travelled widely over the course of my career, this book is decidedly not a travelogue.

I can summarize my life's work as describing, understanding, and striving to improve the health of northern peoples and communities, Indigenous and non-Indigenous, in Canada and other circumpolar countries and regions. I think I did well in describing and understanding, but my goal to improve lives remained unfulfilled. I believe telling this story could play a role in inspiring Canadians to look beyond their own communities and learn about other peoples and cultures, and when possible, to seek out opportunities to make the world a better place for all.

My modest origins and childhood experiences in Hong Kong undoubtedly shaped my outlook in life and my sense of social justice. Aspects of British colonialism and Chinese communism dominated Hong Kong society during my youth. Today I look at the political turmoil in Hong Kong with a sense of loss and outrage. In the late 1970s I undertook for the first time a personal trip to post-Mao China. While fulfilling a long-term dream, the trip also dashed my enthusiasm for the regime. I was disillusioned by what I observed.

I graduated with a degree in medicine in 1973. My first job as a family physician was in a community clinic in Regina, which provided me with a taste of the conflicts that can arise between the medical profession and the community it serves. My job also included weekly visits to the provincial prison, where over sixty percent of the inmates were Indigenous; this was my first introduction to a marginalized segment of the Canadian population.

In 1974, while an intern at the Toronto General Hospital, I attended a lecture about the University of Toronto's outreach health project among First Nations in northwestern Ontario—the "Sioux Lookout Zone." It ignited a spark that led me down a lifelong journey into Indigenous health, as a practitioner, administrator, and researcher. I participated in providing health care to scattered, remote Indigenous communities, and was able to recognize the strengths and weaknesses of the prevalent healthcare system and its underlying government policies. Later, as medical director of the Zone during the early 1980s, I was eyewitness to the emergence of

Indigenous self-determination in health care.

In 1979 my newlywed wife Valerie Dorward and I headed to Tanzania to work for CUSO, a Canadian international development organization. There I engaged in training rural health workers. Tanzania was justifiably proud of its achievements in making primary health care accessible to all in a low-resource environment. The comparison between the Canadian North and the "Third World" is often made. Northern and Indigenous communities experience serious health disparities compared to the rest of Canada, yet the financial and human resources available would be the envy of health ministers in most lower- and middle-income countries (LMICs). While our North is not "as bad" as LMICs, the question that should be asked is, "Why can't we do better? Why do inequalities still exist?"

After Tanzania, I participated in development missions to the Philippines, Zimbabwe, and India as a health consultant, which enabled me to further my interest in Global Health.

From 1983 onward, I became a full-time academic, rising through the ranks at the Universities of Manitoba, Toronto, and ultimately Alberta. I provided a somewhat irreverent look inside academia, especially in senior administration. Much of this time I was engaged in research into Indigenous and northern health in Canada and the circumpolar regions, focusing on strategies to improve health-system performances and the prevention of emerging chronic diseases such as diabetes. I also led a program at U of T devoted to the training of the next generation of Indigenous researchers. I made my final career move in 2013, when I served as Dean of the School of Public Health at the University of Alberta until 2018, retiring at the age of seventy

My research enabled me to make frequent forays to north of 60 in Canada, and later to the northern regions of the planet, including

Alaska, Greenland, the Nordic countries, and Siberia. I also visited non-Arctic regions in the Brazilian Amazon and Australia and compared their Indigenous health systems with ours. My most memorable experiences were my visits to the Chukotka region in the extreme northeast of Russia, both before and after the dissolution of the Soviet Union.

In Canada, my last major research project was the Inuit Health Survey, which took place on the icebreaker *Amundsen* over two summers, in 2007 and 2008. The research vessel traversed the Northwest Passage from Tuktoyaktuk in the west to Labrador in the east, visiting coastal Inuit communities. Beyond the stark beauty of the land and sea, I sensed the fragility of the Arctic. My greatest achievement was helping the development of northern research centres based in Yellowknife, Iqaluit, and Whitehorse, repatriating health research to the North.

This has been a preview of my life story recounted in the following chapters. Why did I embark on such a career? This is a question that colleagues, friends, and students often ask me. Frankly, I do not have a clear answer. I did not sit down one day and list the things I would like to do in my lifetime. I do admit that there was an element of adventure-seeking and wanting to see the world, especially the out-of-the-way places. There was also an element of altruism—how could I best use my education and skills to benefit people, especially the marginalized and underserved? My whole life has been one long, cross-cultural journey—that is a reward in itself. My career prospects certainly did not suffer because of this journey, which did not require any personal sacrifices or serious hardship on my part.

As a long-term observer of Northern and Indigenous health in Canada, I have often been asked if I have seen much progress. Progress has indeed been made, which can largely be attributed to the resilience of Northern and Indigenous people and communities. Yet serious social and health problems persist, and at times seem intractable. I shall, however, close on a note of optimism.

As an educator, I have been encouraged over the years by the increasing number of Northerners—both Indigenous and non-Indigenous—seeking advanced training in the health sciences. On completion of their training, many have returned home to contribute to improving the health and well-being of their communities. I have also observed that Northern and Indigenous trainees often bring their unique, authentic, lived experiences and expertise to the classrooms, enriching other students and instructors. Another trend I have observed is the increasing number of southerners—both Canadian-born and recent immigrants—who are eager to learn first-hand about health conditions in the North and seek opportunities to devote part of their training there. This two-way flow of ideas and mutually respectful co-learning can only hasten the decolonization of education, practice, and research among northern and Indigenous peoples and communities.[1]

1 These final thoughts are quoted from my foreword to Health and Health Care in Northern Canada, edited by Rebecca Schiff and Helle Møller (University of Toronto Press, 2021).

2.

A Hong Kong Childhood

I was born in Hong Kong, on July 7, 1948. My birthday is easy to remember, since 7/7 has a special significance in Chinese history. On July 7, 1937, Japanese troops poured across the Marco Polo Bridge (*Loukouchiao*) in Beijing and ignited the Second World War in China. In the late 1970s, Valerie and I went to work in Tanzania, where we learned that Saba-Saba Day, July 7, was a national holiday.

My first home was No. 5 Haven Street, second floor. I was delivered by a midwife in her home on No. 1 Haven Street. My mother was gravida ten, and by any definition hers would have been classified as a high-risk pregnancy. It is perhaps natural that years later I became an ardent supporter of midwifery and home births. I am the youngest of eight children, with six sisters and one brother—thus I grew up in an overwhelmingly feminine home environment.

One could say that Hong Kong in the 1950s was in its pre-modern stage, before the age of glittering skyscrapers. Our street was wide, lined with three-storey flats on both sides, and in the middle of the street there were tall poinciana, or flame trees, with their bright orange-red flowers. It was in the eastern part of Hong Kong Island, in a district with the incredibly English name of Causeway Bay. In Cantonese, it is called Tung Lo Wan, meaning "Copper

Gong Bay." Causeway Bay is known today particularly for Victoria Park, the site of an annual vigil by tens of thousands of Hong Kong people to remember and protest the Tiananmen Square massacre in Beijing on June 4, 1989, when tanks of the People's Liberation Army rolled over peaceful student demonstrators seeking a democratic China. I was a young boy when Victoria Park was built and was among the first to take advantage of its green space, going there every chance I could to run free and swim in its pool. It has long been my wish to return on June 4 to join the candlelight vigil, but alas, that is not likely to happen. Public recognition of the massacre is illegal in China, though it was only banned in Hong Kong in 2020, under the pretext of the COVID-19 pandemic. The vigil has never been allowed to take place again.

Context is everything, or so my social science colleagues never fail to remind me. A brief digression into some background on Hong Kong is needed at this point to understand how it shaped my formative years. Hong Kong was a British Crown Colony until 1997, when it was "returned" to China under the so-called "One Country, Two Systems" arrangement. China under the Manchu dynasty lost the First Opium War to the British and ceded Hong Kong in 1842, supposedly in perpetuity. Later, Britain acquired Kowloon and the New Territories on a ninety-nine-year lease, after another bout of gunboat diplomacy. That lease ended in 1997. As a child, I considered the colonial status of Hong Kong a source of shame and resentment, and I longed for Hong Kong to become Chinese again. Now, decades later, I count myself lucky to have been born in Hong Kong. Had I been born forty kilometres to the north, inside Chinese territory, my life would have been completely different, if not ruined. While the colonial education system in Hong Kong discouraged one from developing any political consciousness, one was free to learn about the world uncensored. The rule of law, the English language, and the world it opened up were some of the benefits of a Hong Kong upbringing. I now avidly follow political developments in Hong Kong and admire wholeheartedly the young people there who protest the erosions of their rights and freedoms, daring to dream of a free Hong Kong. Six months after the Tiananmen Massacre in 1989, I wrote an op-ed in the *Winnipeg Free Press* about the future of Hong Kong. I compared returning Hong Kong to China to returning a foster child to their biological parents with a known history of child abuse.

My family originated from the village of Shekki, in the county of Chung-san, in the province of Kwantung. The village was situated across from Hong Kong on the west side of the Pearl River Estuary. I never visited it. A famous son of Chung-san was Dr Sun Yat-sen, founder of the Chinese Republic, who overthrew the Manchu dynasty in 1911. Today, the whole Pearl River Delta is one urbanized megalopolis. In Hong Kong, whenever I had to fill in a form, I would enter "Kwantung, Chung-san, Shekki" in the slot for "origin." Even if one was born in Hong Kong, there was always an ancestral village that one could trace one's lineage back to. It is only in the last few decades, long after I left, that I became aware of the emergence of a Hong Kong identity, something that China could not tolerate.

I believe my parents moved to Hong Kong in the 1930s. My father, Kwan-Mo, was born in 1900 and my mother, Koon-Ying, was five years younger. My knowledge of my parents is sketchy at best, and I missed the chance to learn more about our family's history from them before they died. I even missed the chance to find out more from my eldest sisters, when they were still alive.

My parents in traditional gowns, Chinese New Year Day, circa 1950s

My father probably attended, briefly, Fudan University in Shanghai, or perhaps only the university's affiliated secondary school. At the age of nineteen he married my mother in an arranged marriage and had to begin making a living and starting a family. On my birth certificate, his occupation is listed as "*shroff*." The *Oxford English Dictionary* identifies the term as one of Anglo-Indian origin. The occupation has something to do with handling money. He worked at the Blue Bird Café, where he was some sort of manager, but not the very top man—we had to visit his boss first thing on Chinese New Year's Day, while my father's colleagues visited us later that day. The Blue Bird Café was a European-style restaurant, located in the centre of the business district, where Europeans rubbed shoulders with members of the aspiring, emerging Chinese bourgeoisie. Once when my mother took me there, we were greeted effusively by the "uncles" who worked with my father. I saw a nice piece of cake in the glass dessert case and proceeded to help myself. My mother was furious—"Never, ever do that again!" I thought, as the boss's son, I could surely help myself in his restaurant. But my father was not the boss.

An anecdote that circulated illustrates the kind of man my father was. Some years after the war, a reporter in Hong Kong reminisced (not fondly) about the days of the Japanese Occupation. It was towards the end of the "three years and eight months"—that was how people in Hong Kong referred to that dark period. The reporter was stuck with loads of military money issued by the Japanese, which everyone knew would become worthless within days. Apparently he stopped at the Blue Bird Café, where a kind man behind the counter not only allowed him to pay in the cursed currency, but also exchanged it for some forbidden HK dollars, which would soon be back in circulation. The reporter was forever grateful. Although we could not confirm the identity of the kind man in the café, we decided that it could only have been our father.

My family chose to stay in Hong Kong during the Japanese Occupation rather than choosing the even more perilous option of fleeing into the interiors of western China, dodging bandits on the road and Japanese bombers in the air. The Japanese invaded Hong Kong in December 1941, overrunning the defending British, Indian, and Canadian troops. Many of the defeated soldiers became POWs and suffered extreme brutality in internment camps. The civilian population in Hong Kong fared better and were spared atrocities like those inflicted on civilians during the Rape of Nanking. My sisters recalled that on several occasions, soldiers rounded up all the residents of Haven Street and searched their homes while they stood outside, fearing for their lives or "a fate worse than death." My sisters all had their hair cut short to look boyish. One of my uncles on his way to school one day was savagely beaten by Japanese soldiers for not showing sufficient deference. My eldest sister, Nancy, who was a teacher, was given a crash course in Japanese and she then had to teach Japanese to her pupils. In the mid-1960s, she was the first in the family to visit Japan as a tourist, and found her language skills rather handy. If I seem to dwell too much on that war, which I had the good fortune to be born after (as a charter member of the baby boom), it is because Japan never did completely admit its guilt in the postwar years. Furthermore, Japan became a victim following Hiroshima and Nagasaki, and the many heinous crimes against humanity and war crimes that it committed across Asia were conveniently brushed aside.

In traditional Chinese society, the father is the provider and disciplinarian whose word is the law in the home. With one's father, there is more respect (and fear) than love of the cuddly type. I was unlucky in that from an early age, my father was ill. I must have been around five years old when he suffered a stroke at work and his colleagues brought him home in a taxi. Although he eventually recovered most of his abilities, he could not work, putting the family in dire financial straits. There were also doctors' and hospital fees to contend with. He died at the age of sixty-one when I was thirteen, succumbing to the effects of the stroke complicated by reactivated tuberculosis. TB had such a stigma that the doctor did us a favour by not listing it on the death certificate. For years afterwards, my mother would say to me, tearfully, whenever I experienced some success like winning a prize at school, "It hurts me so much that your father is not here to see you now." Because of his illness, I was the only child who did not benefit from his swimming lessons. My sister Kitty told me that our father often took her to the public beach at the west end of the island, and on the way they played a game of mental arithmetic with the numbers on the tram tickets. Despite girls vastly outnumbering boys in our family, which in traditional Chinese society was considered a disaster, my father always believed in education and sports for the girls. I am envious of the good times my siblings were able to have with him.

On my mother's lap, happy and secure

I still dream of my mother, forever loving. One characteristic sums her up best: devotion to her family. It is an eternal regret of mine that between the age of eighteen, when I left home for Canada, and her passing in 1989, I spent only brief periods of time with her. With my career and my own family taking precedence an ocean away, I never realized that one needs to make time for spending with parents until one day it suddenly becomes no longer possible. My mother had a hard life. With so many children and my father being ill, making ends meet was a constant struggle. For some reason, the figure two hundred dollars remains stuck in my mind. It seemed that at the end of each month, my mother would be short two hundred HK dollars. I once found her sobbing in the kitchen over the shotage. What can a little boy do but try not to add to her troubles?

I have fond memories of visiting relatives with my mother, my hand in hers, all over Hong Kong and Kowloon. My mother believed strongly in keeping up relations even with distant relatives.

We would drop in unannounced (as was customary), always after suppertime, when we would be served tea and cakes. The part I did not like was how old people compared their children. "Ah, your son has grown so much and is doing so well in school—mine on the other hand is so lazy," and so on. There were times when we missed the last ferry across the harbour and had to hop into one of the motor launches, called *walla-walla*, that bobbed over the waves, dodging the looming ocean liners.

My mother went to school in her home village up to the end of secondary level. It was a time when Western-style education, and girls' schools in particular, were new-fangled ideas in rural China. She had some English, which stood her in good stead years later when she passed the English test to obtain Canadian citizenship. (We coached her, of course, and she managed to memorize the names of all ten provinces). After her family, the church was my mother's life. We belonged to the Church of Christ in China, an alliance of foreign missions—but predominantly Presbyterian that was formed in China in the 1920s. She was a stalwart member of the women's group in the church, where she made her closest lifelong friends. Her dim sum and other dainties were a legend at church receptions. She was the doer of things away from the limelight, more Martha than Mary. My mother's side of the family had converted first. My father was not much of a believer, I suspect. His views were pragmatic—"Go to church and you'll learn to sing in the choir, read the Bible, and practise public speaking," he would say. "But behave, don't make a noise during the service." I was active in the choir and youth fellowship, which kept me away from behavioural hazards during my teen years. I even taught Sunday school one year.

My mother had a strong Shekki accent, which was the subject of some good-natured ribbing by her younger children and their friends. My aunts, uncles, and grandmothers all had that accent.

Cantonese as spoken in Hong Kong is the urban provincial standard, though almost every village across the province has its own dialect. In the melting pot of Hong Kong, it was possible to pinpoint someone's village from their accent. When speaking to my mother, my two eldest sisters would switch to the Shekki dialect, much to the younger siblings' amusement. There are words and phrases in the Shekki dialect that cannot be translated into standard Cantonese, just as there are Cantonese phrases that have no equivalents in Mandarin. There was a department store in Hong Kong where the employees of an entire floor spoke in the Shekki accent, simply because the floor manager was from Shekki and nepotism was how one got a job in those days.

My mother's life took a turn for the better after my father's death and the consequent easing of the financial burden. In her later years she was able to travel widely to Canada and Australia to visit her far-flung children and grandchildren, and to China to visit her brother Shouqi in Chengdu. He was beaten up by Japanese soldiers, an incident that made him a lifelong anti-colonialist and communist.

Lei Shun Court, circa 2010, before its demolition

Three generations lived in our home on Haven Street, where there were three-tiered bunk beds for the children. In the 1950s, our home was a waystation for relatives coming out of China seeking a better life. Years later, I watched as wrecking balls and bulldozers demolished the old houses on Haven Street one by one, to be replaced by high-rise apartment buildings. We actually moved into one of them—Lei Shun Court on Leighton Road, a ten-storey building in more or less the same neighbourhood as our old house, which has lasted well into the second decade of the new millennium. Our two-bedroom apartment in Lei Shun Court was densely packed, although there were more crowded homes in Hong Kong than ours. During much of my time in high school, I either slept on the dinner table or the sitting room couch. The crowding eased when old people started dying and my sisters left home to be married or to study in Canada. I visited my mother in the Lei Shun Court flat for the last time in 1988, with my young family. As we left, my mother walked us to the elevator, with tears in her eyes, knowing full well that it would likely be the last time we were together.

I never knew my grandfathers. Only after many years in Canada did I find out that my Grandfather Li, my mother's father, had at some point in his life lived in Victoria, British Columbia. He was born after the construction of the Canadian Pacific Railway during the 1880s. Was he in Canada, I have often wondered, during the period of the notorious Chinese Exclusion Act, which was in place from 1923 to 1947? This federal law prohibited outright Chinese immigration to Canada, superseding earlier laws that greatly discouraged immigration through an exorbitant head tax. Did he work in a laundry? None of us knows, and there is no one left to ask. I am convinced that he led a miserable existence in Victoria's Chinatown, suffered blatant racism on a daily basis, and worked to the bone to save enough money to go home and settle down with his family.

Of my father's father, I know even less, not even his name.

I had two grandmothers—Grandma Li on my mother's side and Por-tai ("prime grandmother") on my father's side. I hate to admit that I favoured one over the other. Grandma Li lived just across from us on Haven Street and I went to visit her frequently; I enjoyed being pampered. Grandma Li could read and write, which was unusual for a woman of her era. She lived to one hundred, give or take a year or two. She devoured the communist Chinese press in Hong Kong avidly, believing every word she read. She was kind-hearted, progressive, and broad-minded.

With Grandma Li

Por-tai, on the other hand, appeared old-fashioned, traditionalist, and even reactionary. Her feet were bound—an unconscionable practice inflicted on Chinese women since perhaps the thirteenth century that persisted until the early twentieth. I remember seeing her unwinding the bindings and exposing her tiny deformed feet.

She never seemed to smile, and constantly criticized my mother and us children. The mother-in-law versus daughter-in-law dynamic, well portrayed in many historical novels and plays, was characterized by much psychological, and often physical, abuse. It was pervasive in traditional Chinese society, especially in the days when the extended family lived under one roof. Though both faced oppression, the mother-in-law had her daughter-in-law as an outlet for her anger. The daughter-in-law, when it was her turn to be a mother-in-law, would inflict the same treatment on her own daughter-in-law.

My dislike of Por-tai was partly because of her attitude towards my mother, which I sensed even as a child. One day, when she scolded me for some misdemeanor, I told her to her face: "I don't like you, I love Grandma Li instead." Oh, what cruelty children are capable of! To my surprise and horror, she burst into tears. In between sobs, she shouted, "You bad boy, wait until I tell your father and you'll get the hiding you deserve." Luckily nothing happened, but I did spend a few anxious hours awaiting my fate.

My siblings' names are as follows:

1. Tze-Yin (Nancy), born 1926, deceased 2018
3. Tze-Kit (Kitty), born 1930, deceased 2014
4. Tze-Wing (Winnie), born 1932
5. Fuk-Hing (Julian), born 1934, deceased 2003
6. Tze-Yau (Yvonne), born 1935, deceased 2022
8. Tse-Chi (Mabel), born 1939
9. Chee-Yin (May), born 1942

In many Chinese families, siblings are numbered and often referred to by their birth order rather than their names. I am known to my nieces and nephews as Uncle Number Ten. Siblings Number Two and Number Seven did not survive their childhood. Little is known about them (one was a boy and the other a girl), nor do the younger siblings remember their names. Their ranks, however, remain fixed forever.

There was a six-year gap between me and Number Nine, May. I am not sure if my birth was an afterthought—surely my mother would have been approaching menopause around that time. But being the youngest in the family had its advantages. Nancy (Number One) and I were separated in age by some twenty-two years. She and Kitty were often mistaken for my mother. The first to enter the workforce, Nancy and Kitty became teachers and were the breadwinners of the family, especially after my father's illness. They each continued to support the family even after they married. Neither of them had children of their own, and they showered their love on their younger siblings. Both rose steadily up the ranks in their careers—Nancy became an instructor of fine arts in a teachers' college, and Kitty became a school inspector in physical education. While neither attended university, they were sent by the Hong Kong government to England for various university courses. In their retirement, Nancy immigrated to Melbourne and Kitty to Toronto. I am forever grateful to them. In 2018, I endowed two scholarships in their memory to the School of Public Health at the University of Alberta, with money I inherited from their estates—one for a graduate student from Canada's North, and the other for a student from a middle- or low-income country.

Due to our father's illness, Nancy, as the oldest child, assumed the role of head of our family in many respects. She was somewhat feared by us and her approval was implicitly sought. I remember that she once slapped my face for something cheeky I said. But then she immediately burst into tears and apologized for what she had done. Kitty was most unusual for a Chinese woman. In her youth, she played semi-professional basketball and competed in matches in Hong Kong and throughout Southeast Asia. She was also a Boy Scouts leader, and eventually became a commissioner. She led Scout contingents to jamborees around the world—we were spellbound by the stories and souvenirs she brought home. Later, in Toronto, she became an avid Raptors fan. At her funeral service, her former Scouts from Hong Kong, all in their sixties and seventies, formed an honour guard wearing their Scout uniforms. I have always been in awe of my sisters, who made such an impact on the lives of their pupils that they kept in contact for years and even decades after their school days.

All eight siblings under one roof, 1956

Winnie (Number Three) married Peter, originally from Shantung province in northern China, the birthplace of Confucius. Interprovincial marriages, let alone interracial ones, were uncommon at the time in China, what with the many linguistic, cultural, and dietary differences among regions. I became an uncle for the first time at the age of ten, when Winnie gave birth to Petrova, who grew up to become a doctor. At last count, I have eight nephews and nieces. Peter was physically impressive, since northerners tend to be much taller than the Cantonese. Many police inspectors in Hong Kong were from Shantung, apparently recruited for their build, to put the fear of authority into the unruly Cantonese. Winnie's family emigrated to Australia in the 1970s. Winnie was my piano teacher. She expected perfection but I was unable to comply.

I did not know my sole brother, Julian, well at all. He went to China when I was still a baby. He sat the entrance exam for Peking University, China's premier university, and was accepted. Since the Communist Party knew best, he was assigned to study the Korean language. Upon graduation, he was posted to be a translator at a fishery research institute. I remember corresponding with him, telling him how many marbles I had won playing with neighbourhood kids. His graduation diploma had the slogan "Serve the People" as a watermark, which I thought was quite a nice touch. He came back to Hong Kong for a short visit in 1956—that was when the eight of us siblings had a picture taken lined up according to birth order, except I, the smallest, who was put in the centre. Julian came back to Hong Kong permanently when my father died in 1961. Maybe at that time he was already disillusioned with the "New China." As I was still an idealistic supporter of the regime (from a safe distance), I thought he had betrayed the country by not staying and helping with its reconstruction. We were able to repeat that group pose of 1956 only once, in 1989, when our mother died.

Julian's reintroduction to Hong Kong society was rocky. He had trouble finding a job, as his Mainland China credentials were scoffed at in Hong Kong, and what good was a degree in Korean? He eventually became a reporter and was quite successful. He even interviewed the Beatles when they toured Hong Kong! After his retirement, he lived alone and began showing early signs of Parkinson's disease. In 1996, I went back to Hong Kong and helped him wind up his affairs and move to Canada. Alas, a few short years later he suffered a stroke and had to be cared for in a nursing home in Toronto. I remember visiting him, with a couple of beers. I wheeled him to a quiet corner in the garden, and the two of us savoured a bit of brotherly bonhomie. He died at more or less the same age as my father, far too early.

Yvonne was largely responsible for my political enlightenment. During my primary school years, she was tasked with picking me up from school, since her secondary school was also in the west end of Hong Kong. We would go home together on the bus. Curiously, we would get off somewhere en route and visit a bookstore. It was one of those communist fronts, full of "progressive" books and magazines, and posters of rosy-cheeked Young Pioneers saluting the Great Leader. Communism seduces the young with promises of equality and justice—"*to each according to his needs, from each according to his abilities*," etc. What's not to like? Yvonne rejected a scholarship to study in Japan, and one morning, after saying goodbye to our mother, she snuck out of the house and took the train to China. My father was furious. This was a case of a young woman eloping with her beloved ideals. She studied at an obscure teachers' college in Kwangsi province, in the backwoods. She was by no means unique at the time—many colonially-educated youths in Hong Kong rushed back to the bosom of the Motherland. Eventually, most returned to the detested colony run by the imperialists, as incessant campaigns in China to root out the ideologically polluted, traitors, and counter-revolutionaries took their toll. Armed with a letter from home stating the perilous condition of our father's health and a return train ticket, Yvonne was allowed to leave the country. A one-way ticket home would guarantee refusal of an exit visa. Honest to her bones, Yvonne told her principal that she did not need a return ticket, as she planned to stay in Hong Kong. The wise and sympathetic principal told her, "Just buy a return ticket."

On returning to Hong Kong, Yvonne had to start from scratch. She rose to become principal of a secondary school and started a family. She obtained her first university degree when already a mother. After retirement she emigrated to Toronto.

Yvonne gave me a diary as a Christmas present when I was eleven, to encourage me to write. Unbeknownst to me, she checked on my diary and even wrote comments, which I found out soon enough! Some of these praised me, while others admonished me for misdeeds that I had dutifully recorded and often even gloated about. That's the problem with having sisters who were all teachers! Yvonne gave me some unorthodox advice about learning English. She told me that it was fine to read Dickens and Hardy, but to get the feel for colloquial English I should read something like James Bond. "Just read to get the gist of the story, without being bogged down by trying to look up words in a dictionary."

Mabel and May are the closest to me in age. It seems I was somewhat of a mascot for them, and there are photos of me tagging along wherever they went. They were movie fiends and used to smuggle me into Roxy Theatre nearby, where I sat between them and watched free of charge. Mabel was the trailblazer in the family, being the first to cross the ocean to Canada. She studied at Acadia University in Nova Scotia and later received her MA in education from McGill. May followed Mabel to Acadia. By the time I decided to study in Canada, I had their footsteps to follow. Mabel and May made substantial financial contributions to my university education, for which I am eternally grateful. By 2000, all of us siblings had left Hong Kong, with six in Canada and two in Australia.

The primary school I attended was called Li Shing Government Primary School, located on the west end of the island. With the postwar baby boom, schools were bursting at the seams. Ours was actually two schools in one, sharing the same building. I attended the morning school. In the afternoon, a new set of pupils and teachers would take our places. My sister Kitty taught in the afternoon school. Many of the teachers had been classmates of hers in teachers' college. As a boy, I was prone to talking back to my teachers, a trait that seemed to follow me even into secondary school ("argumentative" and similar descriptive terms appear in a few of my report cards—I have kept them all these years, perhaps as a badge of honour). One time, I so irritated my teacher that she threatened me with the words, "I am going to slip a note on your sister's desk in the teachers' room. She will know all about your misbehaviour when she comes in the afternoon."

My cohort in primary school was one that was experimented upon with early introduction to English, right from Grade 1. My memories of my school days are mostly happy. Corporal punishment was not condoned officially but some teachers still practised it. One big and tall teacher, I recall, was especially vicious. He would smash a ruler on some miscreant's outstretched palm, not infrequently breaking the ruler. I liked my geography teacher the best. Once, I drew the world map on a ping-pong ball and showed it to him; he praised me to the sky.

At the end of Grade 6, all pupils in Hong Kong had to sit a colony-wide exam, the results of which decided which secondary school they would be assigned to. I did reasonably well but was assigned to a technical vocational secondary school, though it was actually quite sought after. Clearly that was not meant for me. My sisters Nancy and Kitty knew what my strengths and weaknesses were, so they spoke to some of their former classmates in the Education Department and were able to switch me to another, more academically-oriented school. In Hong Kong at the time there was a definite hierarchy of secondary schools. At the top of the heap were the government-run King's College and Queen's College; graduating from either would almost guarantee admittance to the University of Hong Kong. The second tier included mainly schools run by the Anglican and Catholic missions. St. Mark's School, where I ended up, was among the lower ranks of this second tier. These were all schools where English was the medium of instruction.

St. Mark's was located in the eastern end of Hong Kong, in a district called Shaukiwan ("basket bay"), a former fishing village. It was certainly not an upscale part of town. Many of my classmates were very poor, and some lived in wooden shacks on the hillside as squatters. They were vulnerable to fires and hurricanes, and water could only be obtained from a standpipe at the bottom of the hill. Secondary school education was not free. There were three classes of fees, depending on family income—$18, $32, and $48 HK per month, if I remember correctly. In the first class of the first day of each month, the teacher would call out each pupil's name, and the pupils would fork over the cash. Everybody knew how much others were paying. Not infrequently, some students could not pay even the lowest amount, and they would be publicly shamed. An insensitive teacher would not hesitate to berate a pupil loudly in front of the whole class. I was in the $48 HK category.

Our principal was Rev Basil Moraes, an Oxford-trained English Anglican missionary who had escaped from China, like many other missionaries in the postwar years. His command of Cantonese was legendary—there was no insulting him in Cantonese behind his back for sure. Though he did not teach us, every once in a while he substituted a class. I was most impressed by the way he found the exact equivalent in colloquial Cantonese for an English phrase. We had a few other foreign teachers, Brits and Aussies. The rest were

Chinese, mainly graduates of the University of Hong Kong and universities in prewar China. Some of them taught in Chinese with only the technical terms in English. The foreign teachers exposed us to "real" English. One advantage of these foreign teachers was that most of the time they could not tell us apart and found our names confusing. Therefore they did not play favourites like some of the Chinese teachers, but evaluated us purely on our exam results. Never a teacher's pet, I won two coveted prizes in Grade 10 and came first overall. I attributed my success partly to the fact that the form master was Australian. I was particularly impressed by one biology teacher, Mr. Affleck, who was fresh out of university. He told us that what we were learning in biology, such as describing the structure of a flower and dissecting frogs, was passé. He said the new biology was molecular, with DNA and the like. This was just a few years after Watson and Crick determined the double helix structure of DNA. My classmates ignored him, since this stuff was not on the syllabus and would not appear in an exam. I, however, was inspired.

Among the Chinese teachers, there were older ones—curmudgeons in my mind—who were conservative and traditionalist. Some had been officials in the Kuomintang government and were virulently anti-communist. Many of my classmates were also refugees from China. There was one teacher, however, who openly espoused pro-communist views, praising the New China at every opportunity and telling us how soon it would surpass the steel production of Great Britain, straight from the *People's Daily*. He was living dangerously, as public discussion of politics was a definite no-no. How times have changed. Today, patriotic education is enforced in Beijing-controlled Hong Kong.

The Chinese population in Hong Kong in the fifties and sixties was bitterly divided depending on whether people supported the Kuomintang under Chiang Kai-shek, hunkering down in Taiwan dreaming of reconquest of the mainland, or the Communists under Mao Tse-tung, plotting to "liberate" Taiwan someday. The two national days were ten days apart—October 1 for the People's Republic of China, and October 10 for the Republic of China. On those days, homes across Hong Kong would proudly hang up the flags of the regime they were loyal to, and it was a bit of a sport to see which side had more flags. The Chinese press was just as divided. For "neutral" news, one had to go to the English *South China Morning Post*, which had its own pro-colonial bias.

My moment of glory at St. Mark's was being selected for the school's quiz team. By then I was already established as a know-it-all, and widely respected by my peers (this is purely my self-assessment). The quiz was a colony-wide contest among schools that aired on the English channel of Radio Hong Kong. We made it to the finals before we met our Waterloo. The question that stumped me was: "What is the name of Queen Victoria's husband?" I prided myself on not learning too much about our colonial masters, and I confused Victoria with Elizabeth I. Thinking it was a trick question, I replied, "She was not married," which brought the house down (I dared not utter the word "virgin"). The next day I was the *bête-noire* of the school. A teacher lamented in class, looking in my direction, "How could anyone not know about Albert, we even have streets named after him!"

Ah, school days were halcyon days. The missionaries were good at educating the whole person, and emphasized not just academics but sports and music as well. We imitated "public" (i.e. private) schools in England, with morning assemblies, houses, school hymns, speech days, sports days, and prefects. The last deserves some mention. It is a well-known trick of the ruling class: let the natives rule themselves, as long as they know who their real boss is. Prefects were given special powers. While we did not endure the physical abuse endemic in English public schools, our prefects issued warnings and noted the names of misbehaving pupils. Accumulated numbers of warnings corresponded with escalated punishments. I was made a prefect one year. It is amazing how a little bit of extra power over one's classmates can be intoxicating.

On August 26, 1966, I left my family, friends, and Hong Kong and set sail for North America. I did not return until 1975, more than eight years later.

What Father Taught Me

Many Canadian men have fond memories of their childhood, being taught by their fathers to play hockey, build a tree house, or ride a bicycle. Growing up in Hong Kong, I did none of these things. Instead, my father taught me calligraphy, a project in which he utterly failed.

Father did not fully recover from his stroke. While unable to engage in my athletic mentorship, he certainly did not neglect the supervision of my intellectual development. For this mission, he adopted a two-pronged (and thoroughly bilingual) approach: making me read to him aloud in English and practising my Chinese calligraphy.

First, the English lesson. I would pick up any English book and read him a set number of pages. He would be lying in bed or sitting up in an easy chair. Most of the time his eyes would be closed, which led me to assume that he was asleep, and thus rush, slur, and skip entire paragraphs altogether. Add to that a child's arrogance—only "modern" young people knew English, and an old man like Father could not possibly understand it. As long as he could hear my voice, the contents did not matter, or so I believed. In retrospect, it was a tribute to Father's tolerance, and indeed playfulness, that my ploy was never exposed. I am forever grateful of this daily ritual that he imposed on me.

The other ritual, calligraphy, was also a battle of wits. Calligraphy is not the same as penmanship. This is calligraphy as practised by the ancients. First, you add water to a slab of inkstone and grind it with an inkstick, creating a slurry-like black ink. I held a gigantic brush that I dipped into the ink, then proceeded to write huge Chinese characters on sheets of newspaper. To do it properly one needed to adopt the right posture, such as the hanging forearm, a very tiring maneuver for a child. Day after day, I wrote and Father watched. He would advise, "a lighter touch here," "more pressure here," and so on. I could not see the value of the exercise, as its resemblance to actual writing with a fountain pen was minimal. I came up with the brilliant idea that if I reduced the supply of old newspaper in the house, my chores would be lessened. So began a clandestine plot to rid the house of old newspapers. Before long, Father noticed the dwindling supply, but rather than launching an investigation, he simply re-used newspapers that I had already written on, the ink having faded after a few days. Not a word was said about the newspapers but I had no doubt that my game was up. Alas, mountains of ink-stained newspapers later, I still could not write with any grace or artistry. So in the end Father lost, but I certainly did not win.

3.

Canada-bound

In the late 1960s, it was still common practice to travel abroad by sea. I travelled on the *SS President Wilson*, an American President Lines passenger liner that plied the Indian and Pacific Oceans, scooping up students between the Middle East and Japan who were bound for higher education in the United States, and of course also new immigrants. At eighteen, I had never left home or travelled outside Hong Kong, not even to the nearby Portuguese enclave of Macau. That my sisters Mabel and May had preceded me already took away much of the fear of the unknown. They had also thoroughly briefed me on Canadian university life, and emphasized that I must take full advantage of the extracurricular activities on offer. I bought one of the cheapest tickets for a bunk bed in steerage, deep in the bowels of the ship below sea level, packed with scores of impecunious students from India, Southeast Asia, and Hong Kong.

The memory of my first morning at sea is permanently seared into my mind. I was having the same dreams that I had in Hong Kong, but when I woke up, it would dawn on me that I was no longer at home. Thankfully there were many diversions. Passengers in steerage spent all their waking hours on deck, savouring new experiences. The ship organized an orientation program on American society and culture for the students and provided us with a chance to practise speaking English with some American professors on board. I was fortunate to have had about three weeks of slow transition at sea, compared to those students who flew, stepping into a brave new world in a matter of hours. I was also able to be met by my cousins in Honolulu and San Francisco along the way.

The last morning on board, at around four am, I was woken up by the person in the next bunk: "We're passing under the Golden Gate Bridge!" Those of us arriving in San Francisco did not get to see the Statue of Liberty, and so our "moment" was travelling under the Golden Gate Bridge instead. I thought about what the future had in store for me—starting a new life in a new country, missing my family back home, going to university, making new friends.

Obviously, San Francisco was not Canada, so I had to switch to airplane mode and flew to Montréal, with a stopover in Chicago. The stopover became an overnight stay on an airport bench, watching my worldly possessions (including a guitar) like a hawk.

McConnell Hall—my very own room, for the first time in my life

I studied at McGill University, where I obtained two degrees (BSc and MD) and remained for seven years. I stayed in residence during my undergraduate degree, at McConnell Hall, which was quite new then. I had a single room to myself. Some Canadian and American students complained about how small the rooms were, but I had gone to heaven! McGill was a favourite destination for students from Hong Kong. In my desire to fit in and immerse myself in the new culture, I deliberately stayed away from other Hong Kong students, who habitually ate together in the dining hall while speaking Cantonese ever so loudly. While I was not exactly rebuffed when I joined the Canadian, American, and British students at their tables, they never seemed to reciprocate. By my second year, I had given up and rejoined the other Hong Kongers. McGill was indeed cosmopolitan, and I met students from all over the world. It was amusing to find out from students from Ghana, for example, that they used the same British textbooks as we did in Hong Kong—clear evidence of Pax Britannica, "where the sun never sets." There was a black-and-white television in the basement recreation room, where I watched the sixties unfold—the Vietnam War, the civil rights movement, Québec's Quiet Revolution, Trudeaumania, etc. I was purely a bystander—I was never in a demonstration, did not go to Woodstock, and pretty well sat out the sexual revolution. I did go to Chicago during the infamous Democratic Convention of 1968. I was there for a reunion of friends from our Hong Kong church, and witnessed the police running amok. At university I had only one goal, and that was to do well academically, to make my parents and siblings proud.

To supplement my income and help defray my tuition and living expenses, I worked every summer and also during the school term. Whenever I had free time, I walked down the mountain into town and checked into an outfit called Industrial Overload. It was an employment agency where one could get a day's work. We job seekers would sit in the waiting room and the foreman would come in, look around, and point. "You, you, and you. The rest can go home." As a clean-cut university student, I seemed to be picked most of the time, but not so the older down-and-outers. I did all sorts of odd jobs and learned about life outside the halls of academia. For two summers I worked at the Toronto Golf Club, thanks to one of Mabel's connections. She had worked there as a chambermaid when she was a student and had made such a great impression that the manager gave me the job when I dropped her name in an introductory letter. The Toronto Golf Club claimed to be the second-oldest golf club in Canada, located just west of Toronto's city limits. It was a very dignified establishment, sedate, with no flashy gimmicks like swimming pools or tennis courts. The membership read like a who's who of Bay Street, and even included a Cabinet minister or two. For my first summer I was assigned to the locker room. The best part of working at the club was serving drinks at the bar and the worst part was cleaning golf shoes. During my first shift at the bar, I gingerly carried a tray of tall glasses of beer, perfectly balanced. But as soon as I lifted up the first glass, the tray tipped. Luckily, the guests were scantily dressed. The second summer I was promoted to the dining room bar upstairs—I had to buy a book on how to mix drinks for that. One day the club secretary, a certain Commander Smith, Royal Navy, retired (like James Bond, but without the panache), called me at the bar and asked me to bring him a cup of tea. I plonked a tea bag in a cup of hot water and brought it to him. His jaw dropped: "You call this tea?" Look, mister, we Chinese have been drinking tea since long before you Brits. One advantage of working in a country club was that the air was good, and we got free room and board, not to mention the staff parties. Unfortunately, we received no tips, as no cash changed hands.

I should mention something about my studies. I enrolled in the honours program in animal behaviour, a decision which caused quite a few guffaws from fellow Hong Kong students, who were all into biochemistry, physiology, and the like, thinking those majors would give them an edge getting into medical school. My program was very interesting, with courses in zoology and psychology, the latter of the experimental and physiological variety, in which McGill was top-notch. By the time I applied to medical school, admission committees were already looking for a somewhat different type of student. I was glad I had studied something more *outré* for my undergraduate degree. I was accepted into the graduate program in neurobiology at the University of Rochester, but declined the offer when McGill's med school accepted me. In retrospect, I don't think I ever had a carefully thought out career plan. Under the British school system in Hong Kong, specialization occurred early on, at least in terms of arts versus science. In the sixth form (pre-university), within the science stream, a further choice was made between the physical and biological sciences. Perhaps my recollection of my father's prolonged illness during my childhood played a role in my decision to go into medicine. The impact of his illness on my family impressed upon me the need for universal, free medical care.

The summer of 1969, with a BSc in hand and waiting to start med school in the fall, I went south to Rehoboth Beach, Delaware, to work in a hotel. It had been advertised as an "idyllic seaside resort" on an attractive summer job poster at the McGill Placement Office. What a rude awakening! First of all, the woman in human resources told me: "Your pay is $200 a month. But if you want to take Sunday off, you'll get a day's pay deducted." In the hotel, the dining room waiters were all white college students, while an all-Black staff toiled in the heat of the kitchen. The chef, which in most establishments would be treated like royalty, had only a tiny loft above the kitchen where he slept, because I believe he was Black.

I, along with two other McGill students, were assigned to housekeeping, not the glamourous dining room. Rent in the seaside town was astronomical, and the three of us shared a basement room with three beds and nothing else. No cooking, and no visitors. As an act of passive resistance, every morning we went to the resort, gathered our brooms and carts, and plonked down on the bed of the first room we entered to catch up on some sleep. At that rate, I would not have broken even by the end of the summer. My salvation came one day when I read in the newspaper that the owner of a local Chinese restaurant had recently been murdered by his chef. His Harvard Law graduate son was coming down from his New York law firm to take over the business. I saw my chance and introduced myself at the restaurant. The son had his old Harvard roommate helping him, although neither knew much about Chinese food or the restaurant business. I looked around and noticed that all the servers were American women. So I said, "How would you like to have an authentic Chinese working as a waiter?" I was hired on the spot. From eight a.m. to four p.m. I worked at the hotel, and from four p.m. to midnight I worked at the Chinese restaurant. The best part was that I got two square meals, at four p.m. and at midnight. While the American waitresses ate their burgers, I got to eat real Chinese food with the owner and the new chef, not the stuff they served their customers. The tips were great, but after a month I was physically a wreck. Again, fortune smiled on me. I received a belated offer from a resort hotel in Muskoka, in the lake and cottage country north of Toronto, and so off I went back to Canada for the remainder of the summer. It was from that hotel's staff room that I watched Neil Armstrong walk on the moon, on a grainy black-and-white TV set.

My Montréal years, from 1966 to 1973, coincided with a tumultuous period in Canadian history. Québec was in turmoil—with the Front de libération du Québec (FLQ), the October Crisis of 1970, and the rise of the sovereignty movement. I certainly gained an understanding of the underlying issues, much more comprehensively than if I had observed the events from afar. I appreciated the francophone Québécois aspiration for self-determination (*maîtres chez nous*) and the need to preserve and protect the French language, but was alarmed by their ethnic chauvinism. On the eve of the Québec independence referendum of 1995 (by then I was living in Winnipeg), I recall going to a concert of the Winnipeg Symphony Orchestra. The conductor—Bramwell Tovey—came out to the podium, turned to face the orchestra, and without a word, struck up "O Canada." There was not a dry eye in the audience. The next day, I took my younger son Robin, nine years old at the time, to The Forks (a historic site where the Red and Assiniboine Rivers join) to attend a huge rally in support of Québec remaining in Canada. I told Robin that it was a historic occasion, and that the Canada we loved might not be the same the next morning if the side in favour of separation won.

The McIntyre Medical Sciences Building, as seen from Mont Royal

I won't dwell on my student days in medical school—quite a few books have been published by doctors lamenting their medical student and intern years. However, I do vividly remember my first class in anatomy when we all met up in the dissection room, amidst rows upon rows of cadavers. Four students were assigned to one cadaver. What an introduction! We were a class of 135. I still have my class photo—not a group photo but a composite of rows of headshots arranged alphabetically. I have done a diversity analysis: the largest group was white Anglo (65), followed by Jewish (41), and Francophone (18), with a smattering of visible minorities—four Africans (from Ghana and Liberia), four Chinese (from Hong Kong and Singapore) and three of Indo-Pakistani origin. After graduation, my classmates were scattered far and wide.

During medical school, I lived in the student "ghetto," just to the east of the McGill campus. It was a neighbourhood made famous by the novels of Mordecai Richler. I recall chatting with a Jewish medical resident at the cafeteria one day, and he asked me what I was reading. When I said Mordecai Richler, he was impressed: "I have never come across a student from Hong Kong who has heard of, let alone read, Mordecai Richler." Looking at the large number of Jewish students in my class, I wondered if some of their parents and grandparents were like the characters described by Richler. Once, I was invited to a Jewish classmate's engagement party at his home. When I showed up, I found that I was the only *goy* and quite an item of curiosity!

Of my professors, there was really only one who had an impact on my later career—Don Bates, professor of the history of medicine, hardly a mainstream subject but one in which I developed a keen interest. We kept up a correspondence after my graduation and he offered invaluable advice on my career development. Later, he became actively involved with the organization Physicians for

Social Responsibility. Inside the McGill medical library is the Osler Library, named after Sir William Osler, considered a father of modern clinical medicine and a bibliophile. That library was my favourite haunt. It has a tremendous collection, not just of medical history but also books on the social aspects of medicine.

I spent the summers of 1970 and 1972 in Europe. In 1970 I signed up for two medical summer schools, one in Edinburgh and the other in three Scandinavian cities—Oslo, Gothenburg, and Copenhagen. These were organized by various student associations, with lectures and even more parties and excursions! It was great to meet fellow students from around the world. I travelled between Edinburgh and Oslo by all manner of transport, but mainly by hitchhiking.

I decided to spend the summer of 1972 travelling in German-speaking countries, ending in Vienna, where I set up a sort of clinical clerkship at the famous Allgemeines Krankenhaus. I had taken an introductory course in German at the Goethe-Institut back in Hong Kong, followed by two years at McGill and a conversational course at the Goethe-Institut in Montreal. Alas, I overestimated my command of the language and was practically useless in the hospital. I did have total immersion in Vienna, as I rented a room in a flat owned by a Hungarian who spoke no English, so we had to communicate in German. He was kind enough to show me around the city. Vienna is rich in medical history. The city is dotted with memorial plaques for Freud, and other famous doctors of the past whose names are associated with diseases, procedures, and treatments that one reads about in medical textbooks. I decided to quit hospital work and instead signed up for a language course at the University of Vienna, before heading back to Canada.

Convocation at Place des Arts, with mother, 1973

I received my Canadian landed immigrant status in 1969. By that time, I had decided that Canada was where I wanted to be for the rest of my life. This status had the side benefit of making me eligible for a provincial bursary, which meant no more part-time and summer jobs were needed, not that there was much room for them in my studies. I became a full-fledged Canadian citizen a few years later, in 1974.

I graduated from medical school in July 1973. My mother, who was living with May in Toronto at the time to help her with childcare, came for my convocation. She was joined by Mabel (then working in Québec's Eastern Townships) and May with her tiny tot Zee-hua. Convocation was a joyous occasion. I hoped that life would be smooth sailing from then on, with no fear of unemployment.

As soon as I graduated, I joined the Anglo exodus down Highway 401 to Toronto, where I began my internship at Toronto General Hospital (TGH). It was wonderful that my mother was close by. An event at TGH led to my lifelong career choice—more on that in the next chapter.

My first job after my internship was as a general practitioner in Regina, Saskatchewan. During my medical student days, I had dreamt of becoming a neurosurgeon—looking back, however, I could not have been more unsuited for it. One day I noticed a newspaper ad mentioning that a recruitment team from the Regina Community Health Centre would be in town. It piqued my interest. Saskatchewan was the pioneer of universal health insurance in Canada, and several community clinics were started at the time of the doctors' strike in 1962, mainly by British doctors who supported Medicare, which was bitterly opposed by the majority of the medical profession in Saskatchewan at that time. These clinics, governed by a citizen board, thrived in several cities in the province. In 1974, a crisis erupted at the clinic in Regina when the entire medical staff resigned *en masse* over a dispute with the board. They set up shop a few blocks away and took all the patients' files with them. The board was left with a building with no files, no patients, and no doctors. They had to start from scratch, which included hiring new doctors. I was adventurous and thought that I would be on the side of the angels with the board against what I considered to be unethical doctors. I was hired, probably the only applicant.

I drove out to Regina in the summer of 1974 and was warmly welcomed by the clinic board and staff. I joined an elderly British doctor who had previously worked in another community clinic. Much of the support of the clinic came from labour unions, cooperatives, and the New Democratic Party. There were hardly any patients to begin with. The local medical community was hostile to our clinic, which in my youthful arrogance I easily brushed off. However, I soon ran into a bit of a storm. I was interviewed by the local newspaper and was quoted, correctly, as saying that I believed doctors should be salaried. I criticized the fee-for-service system of physician remuneration. Subsequently I received a threatening phone call from a local physician and there was a nasty note posted in the doctors' changing room at the hospital. Getting someone to sponsor our application for hospital privileges was problematic, but it eventually came through.

To keep the doctors busy, the clinic contracted with the provincial correctional centre to provide one morning a week of "sick parade." It was an incredible experience. The inmates were incarcerated for relatively minor offences, with sentences of less than two years. Over half of the prison population was Indigenous, yet another indictment of the social conditions prevailing among Indigenous people. (Sadly, decades later, the situation has not changed much). The inmates enjoyed having the chance to see a doctor. Once in a while, an inmate would swallow a razor blade wrapped in toilet paper, which merited a trip out to the hospital emergency room, often requiring surgery. When I left the clinic, many inmates signed a very nice *bon voyage* card.

I stayed at the Regina clinic for only a year. I left not because I did not enjoy the work, but because I received a phone call from Gary Goldthorpe, the zone director in Sioux Lookout, who told me that there was now a vacancy for a GP. After my earlier exposure to working in First Nations communities while an intern at TGH (see next chapter), I had always wanted to work there as a full-time staff physician. Without a second thought, I took up the offer. Sadly, I had to say goodbye to the folks at the clinic. My year in Saskatchewan showed me what Prairie hospitality was like, and it would not be long before I returned to Western Canada.

4.

Northern Exposure

How and why did I spend almost my entire academic and professional career in Neorthern and Indigenous health? It all began one day in 1974 at the Toronto General Hospital, where I was doing my internship, when I walked past an auditorium in which a presentation was underway. A medical specialist had just returned from a short visit to the Sioux Lookout Zone in northwestern Ontario. He talked about the work, the breathtaking landscape, and the people. I was captivated. This chance encounter ignited a spark that led me down a long and rewarding path. An opportunity soon arose, as I had a rotation in family medicine coming up. I sought permission to spend it in Sioux Lookout rather than in the super-specialized Toronto General Hospital. At the time, I had never been to a small town, let alone a village in the bush. In Hong Kong, my knowledge of Indigenous peoeeple in the Americas was acquired from Hollywood movies, but my child's sense of justice was always on the side of the Indians and not the cowboys or the US Army, who invariably won.

The University of Toronto Sioux Lookout Project was the brainchild of Harry Bain, physician-in-chief at the Hospital for Sick Children and a professor of pediatrics at the University of Toronto

(U of T). In the early 1970s, faced with its inability to recruit qualified medical officers to staff its "Indian hospitals," the federal health department turned to Canada's medical schools for help. They were contracted to recruit general practitioners to work for one or more years, supply pediatrics and family medicine residents for monthly rotations, and arrange periodic visits by various medical and surgical specialists. U of T was allocated the Sioux Lookout Zone in northwestern Ontario. The Baffin Zone in the eastern Arctic went to McGill, Keewatin Zone in the central Arctic to the University of Manitoba, the Inuvik Zone in the western Arctic to the University of Alberta, and the Moose Factory Zone in northeastern Ontario to Queen's University.

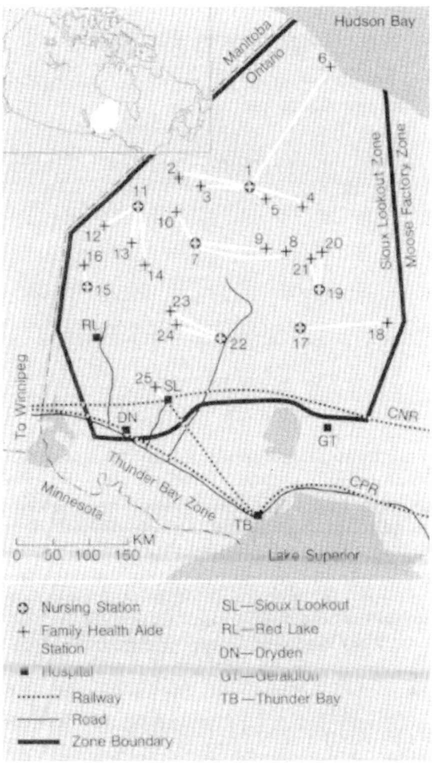

The Sioux Lookout Zone

The Town of Sioux Lookout is located on the transcontinental rail line of the Canadian National Railway in northwestern Ontario, between Thunder Bay and Kenora. It had a population of about 3,000 people, predominantly non-Indigenous. To its north were some twenty-five odd First Nations communities, extending all the way to the shores of Hudson Bay, with a combined population of around 15,000. Culturally they were Swampy Cree, Oji-Cree, and Northern Ojibwa (Anishinaabe). These communities constituted the Sioux Lookout Zone with its headquarters in the Zone Hospital in the town. Travel was conducted by small floatplanes in summer and ski planes in winter, and communication by high-frequency radio.

To really appreciate this vast, seemingly unchanging region deep in the subarctic boreal forest, one needs to take to the skies in a small plane and fly over the endless forests, punctuated by numerous lakes and swamps, and criss-crossed by rivers and streams. Alternatively, one can see the land up close by canoeing down one of the four major river systems (Severn, Winisk, Attawapiskat, and Albany), watching the trees getting smaller and more sparse as they flow north and eventually drain into Hudson Bay.

There were two small hospitals in the town: the seventy-bed federally run Zone Hospital (which opened in 1949 and was originally named Indian Hospital) and the smaller General Hospital serving the townspeople (which opened in 1921). Despite years of talks and negotiations between different levels of government, it was not until 2010 that an amalgamated modern hospital opened—the Meno Ya Win Health Centre—to serve both the town and the outlying First Nations communities, with a broadly representative governing board.

My initial short stint as a visiting intern so captured my imagination that I applied for a full-time position. A vacancy became available in 1975, and I made my way back to Sioux Lookout, having spent the intervening year at the Regina Community Health Centre, as described in the previous chapter. There were four general practitioners on the project then, all recent graduates. The rule was that unmarried doctors served two weeks out of four in the communities, while married doctors had to serve only one. We looked after in-patients in the hospital the rest of the time, but it was the community visits that were the high points of our work. The dentists, on the other hand, spent several weeks at a time in the communities before returning to base.

The Zone Director, Gary Goldthorpe, became my lifelong friend and mentor. A physician with public health training, he had served in the jungles of Malaya working among the Aboriginal people there. He was largely responsible for encouraging me to focus my career on the health of Indigenous people in northern, remote communities. The Zone was a rare example in Canada where primary care, hospital care, and public health were all combined under one administration.

A "medevac" helicopter landing outside the Zone Hospital

While all hospitals conducted mortality reviews, we performed ours with a different approach. Instead of focusing only on deaths within the hospital, Gary directed us to also look at deaths in the communities before the involvement of the health care system. Thus, we looked at social and environmental factors that led to the deaths, and discussed potential preventive measures. Injuries and violence accounted for over a third of all deaths. While some of these could have been prevented by timelier medical interventions, that they occurred in the first place was the outcome of the underlying grinding poverty and cultural dislocation. However, these conditions did not exist uniformly across all communities.

Pikangikum Nursing Station seen from the air, circa 1976

The backbone of the health care system in the Zone were community health nurses (CHNs) working in what were then called nursing stations. Each station would have between two and five CHNs. In the 1970s there were five stations, located in the largest communities. Over the years, the number increased to keep pace with population growth. I had the utmost respect for the nurses working in these isolated outposts; their work could be extremely stressful given the variety of medical conditions that arose, many of which were very serious. The background of these nurses varied. The younger ones were recent graduates, part of whose nursing education included physical assessment of patients. An older group of nurses were British-trained midwives, whose skills were particularly needed. One nurse, originally from Trinidad, was a battle-tested nursing officer in the British Army, with the rank of captain. A regular hospital nurse could not simply be transplanted to a nursing station, where they would be expected to function as a substitute physician. In the 1970s, nurse practitioners were still a relatively new concept in primary care. There were a few shorter-term programs that trained outpost nurses, and the Sioux Lookout Zone was in fact a training site for one such program operated by Dalhousie University in Halifax. Many of the program's graduates subsequently worked at nursing stations across Canada's North.

Even though there were call schedules, in reality everybody was on call all the time. Those were also the days before there were dedicated air ambulance services with trained paramedical staff on board, which did not become fully operational until the mid-1980s. Consultations with a physician at the Zone Hospital in Sioux Lookout were by radio: advice on clinical management was given, or a decision was made to evacuate the patient, called a medevac. However, adverse weather conditions and short daylight periods often meant that very ill patients could remain stranded in the nursing stations for several days. In the 1970s, few communities had airstrips for larger turboprop planes to land. In many communities, break-up and freeze-up were danger periods lasting several weeks, during which neither float nor ski planes could land on the lakes near which the communities were situated. At those times a very expensive helicopter had to be chartered. Although all pregnant women were sent out to the hostel near the Zone Hospital at around the thirty-six-week mark to await deliveries, there were many occasions when deliveries had to be performed in the nursing stations. Many women were rightly reluctant to leave their homes and communities, especially if they had young children. Some would deliberately misinform the nurses about their last menstrual period, leading to a miscalculation of the expected due date, and the delivery would then take place in the community rather than in the hospital.

Family health aides (FHAs), Indigenous health workers from the communities, also played an indispensable role in the Zone. They were predominantly women, often grandmothers, who provided minor treatments in the smaller communities that acted as satellites of nearby nursing stations. They assisted the nurses when they visited, but for the rest of the time they were on their own, with only the radio to connect them to a nursing station for advice. Because the populations were small, the frequency at which serious emergencies occurred was thankfully low. Many of the FHAs had been trained earlier in short courses organized by the federal Department of Health. Their skills improved over time through on-the-job experience. It was a delight to work with these FHAs, who knew their communities intimately. Given the high turnover of physicians and nurses, it was the FHAs who provided continuity of care. They were well respected and were on call, single-handedly, day and night. They were also underpaid and not always appreciated by formally trained physicians, nurses, and administrators. Early on, I was introduced to Margaret Gray in Cat Lake, one of the communities that I was assigned to and regularly visited. She taught me much about the community and the people, their sorrows and their triumphs. The community loved her so much that when a new health centre was built later in the 1990s, it was named after her.

Baby delivered in a nursing station safe and sound

There was another cadre of Indigenous health workers called community health representatives (CHRs), who were predominantly male and worked in the nursing stations. They focused mainly on health education and assisted the environmental health officers in monitoring water quality and sanitation. Since the 1980s, FHAs and CHRs have been merged into one single category, all referred to as CHRs, with standardized training. As more nursing stations were built in former satellites, the need for FHAs was deemed to have lessened. Perhaps this was a deliberate attempt by the government to deny that FHAs were providing clinical care in a legally grey area—the same issue also applied to the nurses. In the 1980s, former Zone physician Elizabeth Roberts and nurse Mae Katt, working on behalf of the Nishnawbe-Aski Nation (the tribal council of regional First Nations), designed a training course for FHAs, filling a critical gap in the health system.

Margaret Gray, FHA, Cat Lake

There were many advantages to working as a GP in a location such as the Sioux Lookout Zone. For recent medical graduates, the clinical experience they acquired could not have been obtained in an urban setting. The Zone Hospital had about 300 deliveries a year, and obstetrics was a major part of our work when we were on call in the hospital. Many of the pregnant women were high risk (not unlike my own mother when I was born), with multiple previous pregnancies. Obstetrics can be both exhilarating and frightening. Bringing a new life into the world and seeing the joy on the faces of the parents are priceless rewards. Yet we often ran into complications. Most of the GPs were also more or less new to the work, with similar training bur lack of experience; there were no experts among us. Fortunately there was an old GP, John Millar, in private practice in town. Originally from Scotland, he had previously served as Zone director in the 1950s and was very experienced in obstetrics and surgery. He was often called in to bail us out of a difficult delivery, especially if a Caesarian section was required. To serve as anesthetists for such occasions, we were all sent out to a non-teaching hospital in Toronto for a month's training in general anesthesia, which was barely adequate. It would have been more effective if the training was provided in another small rural hospital with anesthetists who understood the conditions and equipment the trainees would be sent back to.

For more complicated surgeries such as severe trauma, there was a general surgeon in Dryden, about a hundred kilometres away by road. I recall one hair-raising experience when I escorted a patient with a bleeding stomach ulcer to Dryden. The only plane available was a cramped, four-seater Cessna 180, and we were tossed up and down by the air turbulence all the way. Both the patient and I were airsick. Clutching his hand in one of mine and holding up the intravenous bottle in the other was all I could do. Thankfully, he survived both the trip and the surgery.

Summer Beaver Lake, a new community established in 1975

Another exciting episode occurred during a visit to a satellite community accompanied by a nurse. In such a community, there was a cabin that served as a clinic room during the day and our sleeping quarters at night. One winter night, the nurse and I heard footsteps crunching snow outside the cabin, which usually meant something serious had happened and we were needed. A young man with poorly controlled epilepsy had gone into status epilepticus, a state of prolonged seizures. We were taken to his home by snowmobile. When we got there, a large crowd had already gathered outside, many of whom were wailing. We fought our way inside the house, which was also full of people and lit only by a Coleman lantern. The patient was on his bed against the far wall, and we had to climb onto the bed, boots and all. I drew up a syringe of diazepam, found a vein in the arm, and injected it more by feel than by sight. The seizures stopped and we all heaved a sigh of relief.

Another time, during a visit to a nursing station, a ski plane was landing on the lake—always an occasion of excitement, with people swarming in to meet the plane in their snowmobiles. One person got too close and was nicked in the neck by the propeller. He was brought to the station amidst much furor. Luckily no artery was cut, and despite the blood-drenched clothes, the bleeding was readily staunched. A close call.

In the 1970s there was no dedicated air ambulance, and we had to charter whatever plane was available in town and pressed into service any nurse or doctor not otherwise occupied. One time a nurse and I escorted a baby in an incubator to the Winnipeg Children's Hospital. We landed on an airstrip in the dark of night and the city ambulance was already waiting on the tarmac. When the baby was safely handed over to the hospital, we took a taxi back to the airport to rejoin the crew and the plane to fly back to Sioux Lookout. But where in the airport were they? In our haste we had forgotten to ask the pilot where we could find him and the plane again. The taxi had dropped us off at the main airport terminal. The nurse and I, both wearing parkas and mukluks, pushed the incubator up and down the cavernous departure lounge, quite lost. In the end, some clear-headed airport staff phoned the air traffic tower and found out where the plane was located, far from the main terminal.

The clinical skills I acquired as a GP were not needed in my later career in public health and academic research. To me, the most valuable experience was my introduction to the First Nations communities I worked in, and the opportunity to learn about their ways of life. In the 1970s, many First Nations people were still engaged in the traditional pursuits of hunting, trapping, and fishing, and most older people still spoke only Cree or Ojibwa. I was most annoyed when I overheard visiting students and interns raving about the "great pathologies" they saw in the Zone. They seemed to have completely missed the point of working there.

Sioux Lookout has a special meaning in my personal life—it was where I met my wife Valerie and where our two sons, Steven and Robin, were born. Valerie Dorward hailed from Arbroath, Scotland, but grew up in the seaside town of Seascale, Cumbria, in northwestern England. Her father was an engineer in the nearby Windscale nuclear plant, which achieved notoriety for a major fire in 1957 and the subsequent radioactive fallout that caused long-term health problems. Valerie graduated from the University of St Andrews's dental school in Dundee, then completed her postgraduate training in oral surgery, receiving the Fellowship of the Royal College of Surgeons of Edinburgh. She was all set to go work in Uganda but put that idea to rest when Idi Amin seized power in a coup. She came to Labrador in Canada instead, where she worked for the International Grenfell Association, an organization serving remote Indigenous communities and isolated outports. Her UK credentials allowed her to work in the province of Newfoundland, but not in the rest of Canada. One way to work around this was to enrol in the final year of dentistry at U of T, as graduation from the program came with an automatic license to practice in Ontario. There she learned about the Sioux Lookout Project, which also had a dental component. She was thus able to fulfill her desire to work in an underserved area, similar to her previous work in Labrador.

One day in 1976, I went downstairs to the hospital cafeteria for my coffee break. Lynn Cappell, the dental hygienist, called me over to her table and said, "Kue, I would like to introduce you to our new dentist, Dr Valerie Dorward." For some reason, even then, I sensed that one day we would be married. I visited Valerie's home one evening and decided to light a fire in the hearth for the ambience. No sooner was it lit than dense smoke started billowing out from under the chimney. I hadn't known that there was such a thing as a damper, which happened to be closed. Not a very good first impression, I'd say.

Sioux Lookout offered a great social life, with young health professionals, most of them single and with far too much disposable income. Each month a new crop of visiting students and trainees came up from Toronto to keep the parties going. For big city diversions, Winnipeg was only a few hours' drive away. There was a bit of a social divide, between the "zonies" and the "townies." Because of our U of T connection, we zonies snobbishly considered ourselves "gown" rather than "town."

The great outdoors was steps away—one could literally ski from one's backyard into the woods and spend hours on the trails. In the summer, canoes and kayaks dotted the lakes and rivers. We even had a clay tennis court at the hospital. Those of us who worked in Sioux Lookout full time could never understand how new medical graduates would want to join the rat race, either going into debt trying to build up a practice or spending long hours in some arduous specialty residency program, with more of the same for the foreseeable future. While only a few of the visiting trainees such as myself devoted the rest of their professional career to northern and Indigenous health, many others gained an understanding of the health and social conditions in Canada's far-flung remote communities. In my later career, I often came across former practitioners and researchers, alumni of Sioux Lookout or of other university-affiliated outreach programs, who I considered my kindred spirits.

Wedding reception, Chinese Palace Restaurant, Toronto, Jan 29, 1979

In the 1970s, there were only a few Indigenous people in the town, some of whom were employed in the hospital, performing kitchen, housekeeping, and maintenance jobs. There was one Indigenous nurse in the entire Zone, a trailblazer. I sensed that she seemed to be always on her toes, under the watchful, and not always approving, eyes of other nurses. There was one First Nation community near the town, called Lac Seul, several lakes away. A few Indigenous people could be seen loitering on the streets in various stages of inebriation, contributing to many people's stereotype of the "drunken Indian." By the 1990s, however, there were many more Indigenous people with professional and managerial jobs in the town, owning cars and homes, creating an emerging middle class.

Towards the end of my two-year term of service, I began to contemplate my next move. While I enjoyed contact and interactions with the people and their communities, I came to realize the limitations of the one-on-one clinical medicine that we practiced. We would fly into a community and see maybe thirty to forty patients that the nurses or FHAs had collected for us. Suppose we were able to double or triple that number—would the community's overall health and well-being get any better?

It was becoming obvious to me that public health, with its focus on the community rather than the individual and prevention rather than amelioration, might hold the answer. I applied for and was awarded a graduate fellowship from Health Canada's National Health Research Development Program, at the time the only funding source for health research and graduate training that was not clinical or laboratory-based. For a thesis supervisor I decided on Robin Badgley at U of T, a preeminent medical sociologist in Canada at the time. He had previously conducted a major comprehensive health survey in the Sioux Lookout Zone and had pioneered the introduction of social science in the medical curriculum. In the 1960s, he had conducted seminal research on the doctors' strike and its aftermath in Saskatchewan. I also sought out U of T anthropologist Robert Dunning, who did field work in Pikangikum, one of the communities in the Sioux Lookout Zone. My thesis was titled *Indian Health Care in Northwestern Ontario: Health Status, Medical Care and Social Policy*. I was awarded the MSc degree in 1979. Valerie stayed on in Sioux Lookout during the time I was studying in Toronto. In January of that year Valerie and I got married. A couple of months after our wedding, we took off for

Tanzania, the subject of the next chapter.

In the fall of 1980, we returned to Sioux Lookout and I assumed the position of medical director of the Zone, while Valerie served as dental officer. We were federal government employees then, although our roles included supervising the medical and dental staff working within the U of T Sioux Lookout Project.

In the early 1980s, the Medical Services Branch of Health and Welfare Canada, which was responsible for First Nations health services in the provinces and northern health services in the territories, was undergoing major changes. Up to that point, the upper echelons of the Branch had been occupied by physicians. As their managerial skills were judged inadequate for the burgeoning bureaucracy, they were replaced by administrative and financial officers who had risen through the ranks. At the zone level, the directors were no longer public health physicians, who were assigned the subsidiary role of medical directors. As medical director, I had hoped to put to good use my training in public health and recent service in a developing country. However, my interactions with senior officials at the regional and national levels convinced me that such knowledge and experience were hardly ever called upon. When TB was mentioned, it more likely referred to the Treasury Board rather than to tuberculosis. The officials were preoccupied with budgets and staffing, rather than with designing and implementing intervention programs directed at the many serious health issues affecting the communities, or strengthening frontline primary care providers. I realized that I was not meant for a career in government.

An important development during my stint as medical director in the Sioux Lookout Zone was the transfer of control. It was a "winds of change" moment. Across the country, Indigenous organizations were clamouring for self-determination in their affairs, including health care. Regional tribal councils began to be formed, many of which created a portfolio for health care. At the Zone level, the health directors of tribal councils in our region began participating in the planning meetings. Some communities were allocated funds to operate programs and manage the recruitment of health staff. The transfer process had been criticized by some academics for being a sham, window dressing, under-resourced, and designed for failure. While some of these critiques were valid, I believed that the transfer was still an important first step.

At one of the all-chiefs community meetings on health care in the Zone, a long-time CHR was called upon to interpret from Cree and Ojibwa. On the second day of the meeting, a First Nation chief spoke at length. When it was the interpreter's turn to translate, she simply said, "The Chief said exactly the same thing as he did yesterday," and then sat down! One endearing characteristic of many of the long-term CHRs was that they were strong women who did not hesitate to speak their minds.

The health-care system in the Sioux Lookout Zone that I have described should be familiar to practitioners and students of global health, as it was and largely still is very much the system in place in much of the developing world. In 1977, the World Health Organization (WHO) promulgated the goal of "Health for All by the Year 2000," which was to be achieved through strengthening primary health care. The deployment of nurses and community health workers as providers of primary care all across northern Canada was in keeping with the Alma Ata Declaration of 1978. In 1981, we were very much excited when Halfdan Mahler, then the Director General of WHO, came to Sioux Lookout for a visit. I suspected many of my superiors in the health department were puzzled as to why we were bestowed such an honour. I supposed Mahler wanted to see for himself how a system promoted for use in poor developing countries was equally applicable to a remote region of a very rich developed country.

In my meetings with Indigenous leaders in the region, I detected a prevalent perception that a system that relied on nurses and FHAs was second class. If the rest of the Canadian population had access to doctors, why didn't the Indigenous people in remote communities? Was this *prima facie* evidence of inequity, or was it the proper use of scarce resources appropriate for small, widely dispersed communities? This was a question that continued to occupy my mind later in my research career. To be sure, there were indeed many instances of poor and culturally insensitive care. Dissatisfaction with the quantity and quality of the services provided culminated in a sit-in and hunger strike at the Zone Hospital in 1988 by several First Nations leaders. I had left the Zone by then. The government responded by appointing a review panel consisting of Archbishop Ted Scott of the Anglican Church of Canada, Grand Chief Wally McKay of the Nishnawbe Aski Nation, and Harry Bain, founder of the U of T Sioux Lookout Project. Among the panel's recommendations in 1989 was the establishment of the Sioux Lookout First Nations Health Authority (SLFNHA), which became a reality in 1990, an important step towards Indigenous control of health care in the region.

In 1983, I resigned as medical director in Sioux Lookout and took up the position of assistant professor in community health sciences at the University of Manitoba, though our family kept up our connections with Sioux Lookout even after we had left. For a few years each summer, I returned to the Zone to serve as a locum GP, renewing my acquaintance with the staff and the communities. This stopped when it became clear that my clinical skills were rusty, as by then I had completely immersed myself in academic teaching and research. However, I was still involved in other capacities, such as the investigation of a TB outbreak and collaboration in diabetes research. My most extensive involvement was from 1993 to 1995, when I was contracted by SLFNHA to conduct a comprehensive planning of regional health services in support of the negotiation process towards the amalgamation of the two hospitals in Sioux Lookout. In 2013, I attended a conference organized by SLFNHA and delivered a keynote address on promoting research in support of health system improvement in remote First Nations communities. A senior manager in SLFNHA was someone I had known for some twenty years and greatly respected. When I was a young GP in the Zone, she was a CHR in one of the smaller communities. Her mother was a CHR in another community. Later on she went to university and obtained a nursing degree, then returned to work in the Zone. Her education and experience were called upon to help get SLFNHA established.

During our Sioux Lookout years, Valerie and I made many lifelong friends. I have previously mentioned Gary Goldthorpe. Another friend was Joyce Timpson, a social worker who first moved to Sioux Lookout and worked for the Children's Aid Society in the early 1970s. In the 1980s she developed and directed a community-based mental health program for the Zone, a much needed and utilized service. Later still she became active in municipal politics in Sioux Lookout.

In 2000, Valerie set up a private dental clinic in Sioux Lookout with Lynn Cappell, a dental hygienist and her long-standing colleague from the Zone. Valerie commuted on weekends from Winnipeg before eventually closing her practice in 2005. Thus, one way or another, we both found ways of staying connected to Sioux Lookout. It holds a special place in our hearts.

Our log home in Sioux Lookout

Nishnawbe-Aski Nation—"The People and the Land"

Rapids in Severn River

A northern lake at sunset

5.

African Interlude

While in Sioux Lookout, Valerie and I were already contemplating where our future lives would unfold. We both wanted to work overseas, in the developing world (subsequently relabelled lower- and middle-income countries, or LMICs). It had been Valerie's earlier dream to work in Uganda, which was thwarted by Idi Amin. We decided to apply to CUSO (Canadian University Service Overseas). Even as a medical student, I had been interested in that organization, which was established in 1961 by a group of Canadian university graduates. By the late 1970s, CUSO's focus had evolved from placing generalist university graduates primarily as schoolteachers to recruiting specialized professionals such as agriculturalists, doctors, engineers, mechanics, etc. After we were accepted, we had to decide on our preferred country to serve in. We narrowed it down to two—Papua New Guinea and Tanzania. I jokingly summarized the decision as: "if we go to Papua New Guinea, it will be because of its anthropology; but if we go to Tanzania, it will be for its politics." Tanzania won out.

Valerie and I got married in Toronto in January 1979. Instead of a honeymoon, we newlyweds soon took off for our posts in Mbeya, southern Tanzania. First, we underwent orientation in Ottawa with other CUSO cooperants (we were no longer called volunteers by that point) destined for the far corners of the globe. We stopped over in London and visited the Institute of Child Health to meet David Morley, an authority on tropical child health. There we ran into John Frank and Eden Anderson, the homeward-bound Canadian CUSO couple whose house in Mbeya we were to occupy; I was also to take over the job that John Frank had held. Our being briefed by them directly was very timely and helpful, and my path and John Frank's were to cross again later during our academic careers in Canada. When we landed on Tanzanian soil, I saw to my surprise that awaiting us was Catherine Oliver, a classmate of mine at McGill. It was amazing that even after having spent four years in the same medical school, we had no idea that we had similar interests in the developing world.

We spent a few days in Dar es Salaam, the capital (hereafter referred to as Dar), sorting out administrative issues with the CUSO office and relevant government departments. Dar was outwardly unimpressive, with few new buildings. There were too many cars, even when petrol was severely rationed and exorbitantly priced. Public transportation was clearly inadequate for the masses, with people clinging precariously to packed buses. CUSO rented a hostel in the tree-lined, upscale Upanga district to house visiting volunteers from the back country. Upanga was a far cry from the overcrowded townships such as Kariakoo, where poor Tanzanians eked out a living.

Before taking up our posts in Mbeya, we spent a month at the Expatriate Development Workers Training Centre in Morogoro learning Swahili, the national language, and underwent some cultural orientation. We were not expected to practise our professions in Swahili, but to learn enough to carry on a conversation and be more aware of our surroundings. Morogoro is a medium-sized regional centre, perched on the scenic Uluguru Mountains about 200 kilometres west of Dar. The centre was located within the grounds of a teachers' college, which also hosted a training program for National Service youths. Our teachers were young and enthusiastic, but were understandably taciturn when conversations veered towards politics. There were about twenty students from various western countries, half of them Canadians.

In addition to classes, we were also sent to the market with a slip of paper indicating what we were to buy using Swahili. We went to a local restaurant and were supposed to learn about ordering food, except there was only one item on the menu. People living in nearby villages were used to seeing foreigners and they were very friendly, enabling us to practise Swahili with them. Similarly, the centre's nightwatchman and cooks engaged us in conversations to our mutual amusement.

The month went by quickly. It felt like a holiday and a reprieve from our hectic travelling getting into the country. The food and accommodation were excellent. We looked forward, not without some trepidation and anxiety, to reporting to our respective posts in different parts of the country, doing different jobs. Married couples were thankfully posted to the same location. Being married was a blessing, as two people were definitely better for overcoming some of the hurdles faced in living and working in a new environment.

I had mentioned that we chose Tanzania because of its politics. In the 1970s, under the leadership of President Julius Nyerere, Tanzania was held up as a shining example of a poor but self-reliant country that had pursued its own distinct path towards development. Countries east and west were eager to shower development assistance on Tanzania. From the east came China, the Soviet Union, and Cuba, and from the west, Canada, the Nordic countries, Germany, the United States, and Japan. There was relatively little corruption and few intertribal conflicts (by African standards), but as a one-party state, it was far from democratic. Nyerere was widely loved and respected by the people, who called him *Mwalimu*, meaning "teacher." His brand of African socialism entailed the nationalization of major industries and the collectivization of agriculture. The latter was implemented through the creation of *ujamaa* villages (*ujamaa* roughly translates to "family" or "community"), a concept not unlike the people's communes in China.

By the late 1970s, around the time of our arrival, Tanzania's economy was in dire straits. The policy of *ujamaa* villages was a failure, despite the forced villagization of peasants. Agricultural production plummeted and there were widespread food shortages. Few consumer goods were produced domestically, and imports were strictly restricted. On top of that, Uganda under Idi Amin invaded Tanzania in 1979, leading to a war that ended with victory for Tanzania and the overthrow of Amin. Early on in the war, some CUSO cooperants working near the border were hastily evacuated just ahead of the invading army. By the time we arrived, the Ugandan Army had already been pushed back across the border.

We were posted to Mbeya in the southern highlands near the Zambian border. At 1,500 metres above sea level, its climate was temperate and comfortably cool year-round. Houses were neatly arranged on the mountainside. The city was surrounded by rich agricultural lands such that fresh fruits and vegetables were readily available—our food supply was the envy of other CUSO cooperants posted to the arid parts of the country.

My job was to teach in a Medical Assistants' Training Centre (MATC). Tanzania's model of primary health care was justifiably praised internationally. MATCs accepted secondary school graduates who underwent a three-year training program to prepare them to work independently in rural health centres. They were called medical assistants (MAs). Most importantly, career progression was built into the system, enabling MAs to be upgraded to Assistant Medical Officers who were eligible to apply to the University of Dar es Salaam to study medicine and obtain an MD degree. In Mbeya, I worked alongside Tanzanian physicians in the MATC. We taught basic medical diagnosis and treatment in the classroom and at the bedside, the latter of which took place in the adjacent regional hospital. Other than taking our turns being on call, MATC teachers did not have any clinical responsibilities in the hospital. These responsibilities instead fell to a team of doctors from the Soviet Union, who were not involved in teaching. It was quite an introduction to Soviet medicine—even with an open mind, I had to lament for the patients under their care. The Soviet doctors tended to overprescribe multiple drugs, especially antibiotics, even when they were in short supply. They actually lived better than we did, as they had access to their embassy for both staples and luxury items. We got along particularly well with one of them, and were once invited to their home for supper, which consisted almost entirely of alcohol. The leader of the Soviet medical team was an alpha female (nicknamed KGB) who tolerated no dissent, and to whom all the male doctors deferred. I did not know then that years later I would visit the Soviet North and examine closely its health care system.

I also designed community health projects for our students, who were sent to rural villages for their practicum. There was a subject in the curriculum called *siasa*, or political studies, taught only by the Tanzanian staff. This was similar to the obligatory courses on Marxism-Leninism in universities in China (where Mao Tse-tung's Thoughts took precedence) and Eastern Europe. On Saturday mornings, all students were required to do manual labour around campus, clearing bush and cleaning floors, which I applauded.

Visiting students at their rural practicum with MATC colleagues

One of my clinical tasks was performing autopsies. They were infrequent and usually for medico-legal reasons. In Canada, this was a task reserved for pathologists, but in Tanzania, all doctors were supposed to know how to do them. The autopsy building had no refrigeration or air conditioning, though a large baobab tree provided much-needed shade. Whenever an autopsy was underway, there would be a large gathering of friends and relatives outside, and the women would be wailing and ululating. Fortunately, there was a very capable morgue attendant who basically told me what needed to be done. It was all gross anatomy, and lab tests were very limited. Once, I had to perform an autopsy on a body which had been carried on the back of a pickup truck from a remote village for hours in the hot sun. Foul play was suspected and the cause of injury was quite obvious. However, I did not know that I had to extract stomach fluid to test for alcohol, and I released the body without doing so. I was severely reprimanded by the regional medical director, and I wonder if my error perverted the course of justice.

Valerie in discussion with her dental colleagues

Valerie's work was entirely clinical. Almost all dental procedures were extractions. In the mornings, a large number of people would already be waiting in front of the clinic. Prior to our departure from Canada, Valerie had collected donated equipment and shipped it to Mbeya. The package got there just fine, but sadly the notice from the post office sat on the MATC administrator's desk for weeks, and the shipment was either returned to Canada uncollected or pilfered.

We had free housing, a two-bedroom concrete bungalow with an aluminum roof. It was very comfortable and all we needed. While lying on our bed, we saw large, brightly-coloured spiders outside the window. When it rained, the cacophony on the roof was deafening, and so was the less-than-elegant landing of ravens and vultures. The market was well supplied with fresh fruits and vegetables, but we did not sample the meat. For that there was Chakula Barafu, a store that sold frozen meat at prices that ordinary Tanzanians could not afford. There was a rice plantation down the highway, funded by the Chinese government. Women sold rice in metal containers called *debes*—the sides were usually bashed in and at the bottom there was often all manner of sand and grit to reduce their capacity (but not the price).

On weekends we went for long walks exploring the town and short hikes up the mountain just behind our house. We treated ourselves to the occasional lunch at the Mbeya Hotel. This establishment was a throwback to colonial days. The veranda overlooked a garden full of blooming flowers. There was a faded mural in the dining room depicting the prowess of big-game hunters in bygone days. The hotel kept to old standards with a full-course menu and silver service, although the servers were dressed in tattered, off-white uniforms.

Our house was often visited by young boys. They knocked on the door and yelled, "Bruce Lee, come teach us kung fu!" Even when walking down the street, kids would follow me as if I was the Pied Piper. For some unfathomable reason, the only movies shown in the town were either Bollywood romances or kung fu flicks from Hong Kong. No decadent Hollywood movies were allowed into the country. I often told Canadian students that to really appreciate what it was like to be a minority, one had to live in a place like Africa, where one would always be an item of curiosity in a sea of Black faces.

Young kung-fu enthusiasts outside our house

CUSO was a decentralized organization, with each country office setting its own policies. Several times a year, all the cooperants from across the country would assemble in Dar es Salaam for a business meeting. It was also a chance to eat in a restaurant, Indian mainly. The meeting was a great opportunity to share stories from our diverse experiences. Steve Gurman was an engineer from Montréal whom we particularly liked, so much so that we named our first son after him—our second son, Robin, was named after Robin Badgley, my professor at U of T. CUSO had a longstanding policy that cooperants should be paid the same salary as their local counterparts, which was quite different from some development organizations that paid home-country wages. Interestingly, the cooperants in Tanzania went a step further toward egalitarianism—we were all paid the same salary, regardless of the job. But not all workers in Tanzania were paid the same salary, and doctors were paid more than teachers. In our case, Valerie and I were in fact paid less than our Tanzanian counterparts, which was a source of surprise to them. They joked that "you Canadians are more socialistic than us!" Nevertheless, with two salaries of 200 shillings a month each and free housing, we lived quite comfortably. We even saved enough to have a beach holiday in Dar, and bathed in the Indian Ocean.

A young patient of Valerie's befriended her and invited us to visit her home village one weekend, further up the mountains near Tukuyu. We stayed in her parents' home, which was simple but comfortable. It was a far better cultural orientation than all the books on Tanzania that we had read. That Sunday, we went to a Lutheran church just as the service was ending. The congregation exited the building and formed a big circle on the grass clearing. They swayed, clapped, and sang the most beautiful hymns I had ever heard. When we left the village, the head of the family grabbed a chicken that was unlucky enough to be strolling by, turned it upside down, tied its legs, and handed it to us as a parting gift! We didn't know how to slaughter a chicken, urbanites that we were. When we got back, we solved the problem by giving it to one of our colleagues who had a kitchen helper who knew what to do.

Our hosts at a village near Tukuyu

My adventurous sister Mabel came to spend the Christmas of 1979 with us, a much-anticipated visit. Having picked her up at Dar es Salaam airport, we stopped by the Mikumi National Park on the way back to Mbeya. We stayed in the wildlife camp rather than the lodge. That night, both Mabel and Valerie had close calls with the wildlife. Valerie sat down on the outdoor privy and heard a hiss—she flew out of the stall like a shot. It was not clear where the snake was. Later that night, Mabel almost walked into a wandering elephant whose body was indistinguishable from the surrounding pitch-darkness. Her visit was marred towards the end when our car was broken into on a street in Dar and all our belongings were stolen. I reported the theft to the local police station and was told outright that I was wasting my time. While I waited, I saw above my head on the notice board an Interpol "most wanted" poster. It showed mugshots of several Japanese Red Army fugitives. I avoided eye contact with the desk sergeant.

Our car was a Renault 4, which we had bought from a departing Danish physiotherapist with money lent to us by the CUSO office. It was the office that actually owned the car, which would be transferred to another cooperant when we left. Under the strict import controls in place then, cars actually appreciated in value as they aged and deteriorated. The roads were atrocious and the lorry and bus drivers were a menace. On the rare occasions when we took a long-distance bus to Dar, our driver amused himself by overtaking and racing with other vehicles, all the while being egged on by the passengers. From time to time the bus stopped for toilet breaks, whenever it suited the driver. For men it was simple—one went *porini* (into the bush). The women, wearing the traditional sarong-like wraparound (*khanga*), managed some distance away with modesty. For expatriate women wearing jeans, however, it was a more complicated maneuver, and one had better be ready when the bus engine started. One CUSO friend had the misfortune of scooping up several burrs into her jeans and had to sit uncomfortably for hours back on the bus.

Being mobile was important to us, as it enabled us to see more of the country. The other mode of transportation was the railway. Mbeya was on the route of the Tanzania-Zambia Railway (TAZARA), funded and built by the Chinese government. TAZARA was our preferred mode of travel between Dar and Mbeya, far superior to road travel by car or bus. The train stations were exact replicas of those I had seen in China, with traditional Chinese architectural designs. There were two classes on the train, with soft seats in first class and hard seats in second. On one journey we met several Chinese engineers and rail workers, all dressed in blue Mao suits. We started a conversation and they pumped me full of questions about life in Canada: Do you own a house? Why are you in Africa? What is your monthly salary? We learned that there was a Chinese man living in Mbeya who had been there for some years; a former gold miner who had stayed on, married an African woman, and started a family. We visited him and he was delighted to see a fellow countryman, which must have been a rare event. Unfortunately, we were not able to develop a friendship, as I soon left the country.

There was a sizable population of Asians in Tanzania, as in much of East Africa. Under the old colonial society, they constituted a "middle class," between the European overlords and the African masses. Post-independence, however, their status became precarious—an extreme example was their expulsion from Uganda in 1972 by Idi Amin. Nothing of the sort happened in Kenya or Tanzania. Although tolerated, the Asians were not particularly well liked, especially since they constituted much of the merchant class and were generally economically better off. Their situation was not unlike that of the Chinese in Southeast Asia. Under policies of Africanization, there was sometimes reverse discrimination in terms of government jobs. There was one Asian student in our MATC who received the highest scores in all subjects. On reviewing the school's academic records, I noticed that the prize for ranking topmost was not awarded to him, but to the student in second place. There was an Asian-owned *duka* in town, where we shopped from time to time. One day, I was asked to go into the back of the shop, where the owner made a proposition. He could give us shillings, of which he had a surfeit, if we promised to deliver the equivalent amount of Canadian dollars to his brother in Toronto when we arrived back home. Such a transaction was likely illegal so we declined, but it was interesting to see the informal international banking system in operation, based entirely on trust. There was an

Asian physician on the MATC teaching staff whom we liked very much. A few years later, we heard that he succeeded in emigrating to England, though sadly, but perhaps not surprisingly, he was assaulted on the street by some skinheads.

My students were a joy to teach. They came from all over the country. There was even a Rwandan refugee who had grown up in a camp in Tanzania. English was the medium of instruction in post-secondary education. The policy of making Swahili rather than English the official national language in Tanzania had been very successful. It was a unifying force in a country where there were many tribal languages. Although it has many Arabic loan words, Swahili is a Bantu language. With the exception of coastal people, Swahili is a second or third language in much of the country. The typical Tanzanian could speak at least two or three languages, if not more, putting unilingual Canadians to shame.

Boisterous celebration on graduation day—after which they would be sent to rural health centres across the country

There was a cholera epidemic during our time in Tanzania. Unfortunately, what the students saw in practice was not what they were taught in class. Some of the knee-jerk epidemic measures taken by the government were not appropriate for cholera, a water-borne disease. Towns and villages were quarantined and vast amounts of perfectly safe fruits (especially the heavenly mangoes) were confiscated from peasants taking their produce to market and dumped on the side of the road. These fruits were so "dangerous" that policemen were seen gorging themselves with abandon. Travel was restricted unless one had a permit. These were mimeographed forms that our students were asked to help produce, which they signed themselves and gave to their friends. An effective health-promotion tool was the popular *khanga* worn by women, which pictured red-and-white tetracycline tablets floating among the cholera bacteria (*vijidudu*).

The typical stint for a CUSO cooperant was two years. I left six months early at the close of the academic year, when I received a letter from Harry Bain urging me to return to Sioux Lookout to assume the role of medical director. In retrospect, it was clearly my career ambition that drove my decision to take up the offer and leave. Valerie was determined to stick to her commitment and decided to stay on a bit longer. She was pregnant with Steven at the time. To our relief, Catherine Oliver, my McGill classmate who was teaching in a MATC in the much smaller and more remote town of Ifakara, offered to move to Mbeya to take over my post and live with Valerie.

Around October 1980, I flew from Sioux Lookout to London to meet Valerie, who had completed her stint in Mbeya. When Valerie stepped out at Heathrow, visibly pregnant, she was wearing a pair of jeans held together by a safety pin. Due to import controls, she had been unable to buy new, more spacious attire. We spent some time with her parents in the north of England before returning to Canada together.

Back in Sioux Lookout, this time as medical director, I had the opportunity to reflect on and compare my experiences working with remote Indigenous communities in Canada and rural communities in Tanzania. In 1983, I published an article in the *Canadian Journal of Public Health* titled "The Canadian North and the Third World: Is the Analogy Appropriate?" In 1986, I also published a paper on "Socialist Development and Primary Health Care: The Case of Tanzania" in the anthropology journal *Human Organization*. It seemed that every job I had I wanted to write about.

I often returned to the theme of the Canadian North and LMICs in lectures and presentations in my later academic career. My main arguments can be summarized in two charts. One shows the global rankings of infant mortality rates, with Canadian First Nations and Inuit ranked against all the countries in the world. It is clear that Canadian Indigenous people rank far worse than the rest of Canada. Globally, they have similar infant mortality rates to countries in Latin America and Eastern Europe, but lower rates than the least-developed countries in sub-Saharan Africa.

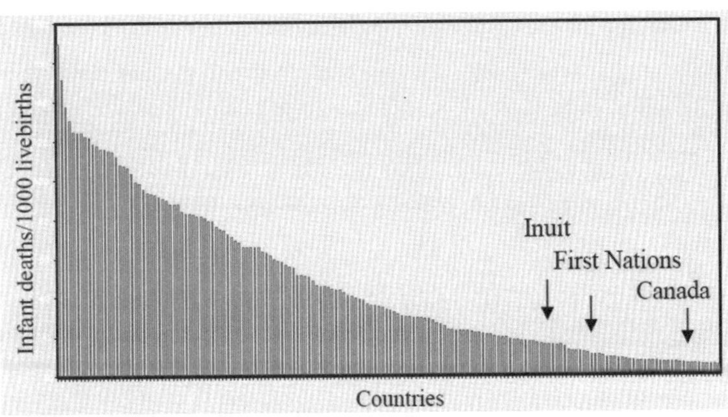

Global ranking of infant mortality rates

The other chart ranks the three northern territories of Canada against all the countries in the world in terms of per capita health expenditures in US dollars. Per capita health expenditures in Canada's North ranked among the highest in the world, in the thousands of dollars, compared to below ten dollars per person per year in many of the least developed countries.

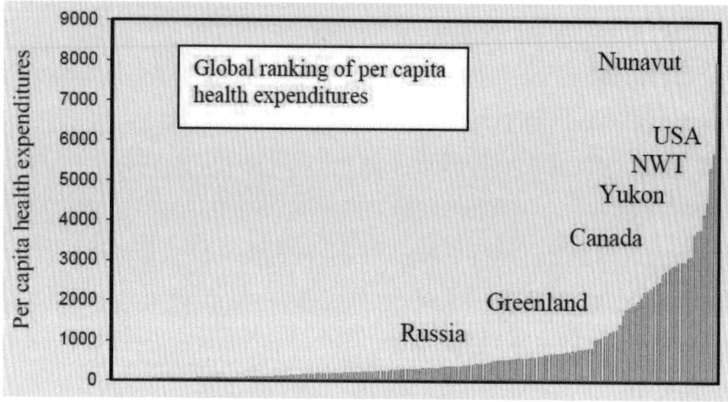

Global ranking of per capita health expenditures

My take-home messages were: Northern and Indigenous communities in Canada experience serious health disparities compared to the rest of the country, yet they cannot be compared to the worst off among LMICs. This does not excuse the Canadian state from the responsibility of improving the health status of marginalized populations. In terms of health care, the financial resources available to northern and Indigenous communities would be the envy of health ministers in LMICs. Contrary to common belief, health care in Canada's North is not under-resourced, but has in fact double (or more than double) the resources of the national average. Though things are not as bad as they might seem, the more important question should be: If Canada is such a rich country and so much money is spent on northern and Indigenous health care, why can't we do better? Why do health inequalities still exist?

I maintained my interest in international health after returning from Tanzania. The experience enriched both me and Valerie. However, my continuing involvement took the form of short-term projects. In the 1980s, while at the University of Manitoba, I was awarded several contracts to serve as a health consultant in the Philippines (1986), Zimbabwe (1988), and India (1989).

Shortly after the 1986 People Power Revolution in the Philippines that ousted dictator Ferdinand Marcos, newly installed President Corazon Aquino approached the Canadian government for urgent development assistance, as the country was near bankruptcy after years of Marcos's extravagant and larcenous regime. The Canadian International Development Agency (CIDA) assembled a multi-sector team of experts in agriculture, forestry, engineering, health, etc., for a planning mission to the Philippines. I was selected as the health expert. There was another physician on the team, Rey Pagtagkhan, a pediatrician from Winnipeg who was president of the Filipino-Canadian Association at the time. As a graduate of the University of the Philippines, he knew all the key people in the country's health sector. He later went into politics and became a cabinet minister in Jean Chrétien's Liberal government. We travelled all over the country, from the north of Luzon to Davao City in Mindanao in the south. We visited community health projects (both rural and urban), health professional training institutions, national and local health authorities, research centres, and non-governmental organizations (NGOs). Essentially, our purpose was to find out where and what the needs were, and in which shape and form Canada's assistance could best make an impact. We were treated as honoured guests wherever we went.

Rural women in southern Luzon, Philippines

The health sector team visited one family in a village to see how the people there lived. The family offered us lunch. We knew that they scraped together what little they had to feed us. This put us in a moral dilemma: to not eat what they offered would be gravely insulting and disrespectful, yet, if we ate too much, the rest of the family would go hungry. We had to strike a delicate balance.

After our field trips, the team reassembled in a luxury hotel in Manila, discussed our findings, and tried to produce a set of recommendations. We also underwent gender sensitivity training. A local NGO that rescued sex workers took us to a notorious red-light district. Each of us was paired with a Filipino/Filipina person of the opposite gender. We posed as tourists and visited bars and clubs. It was a very depressing experience, seeing scantily dressed young women gyrating on the stage and serving a lascivious, inebriated, and mostly European clientele. Outrageously, the next day, some of the male CIDA team members joked and smirked about the evening's "sights," completely missing—it seemed to me—the point of the visit. The NGO had wanted the Canadians to see for themselves the degradation of women in the sex trade and to understand that the cash-strapped NGOs were in need Canadian assistance to the Philippines. I do not know the outcome of our planning mission, whether any of our recommendations were translated into concrete support. Such was the nature of being a consultant—travel, look, return, and write a report on what's good for the people. It was a positive experience, however, and I welcomed more such consultancies.

In 1988, I went to Zimbabwe on behalf of the Canadian Public Health Association, which had provided substantial support to that country's Expanded Program of Immunizations (EPI). My role was to check on the progress of various projects, but also to participate in the training for and implementation of a national immunization survey.

Immunization survey in Masvingo district, Zimbabwe

The white minority government in the former Southern Rhodesia had unilaterally declared independence from Britain in 1965. A bitter and bloody civil war ensued, culminating in the multiracial parliamentary election of 1980, which saw the success of the Zimbabwe African National Union (ZANU) under Robert Mugabe. Valerie and I were still in Tanzania at the time and witnessed widespread jubilation among Tanzanians. By the time of my visit to Zimbabwe in 1988, Mugabe was still feted internationally as a great leader, although signs of human rights violations against political opponents were already evident. Mugabe became increasingly despotic and ruled Zimbabwe for thirty-seven years until his ousting by a military coup in 2017. Interestingly, Mugabe himself was on the same flight to Zimbabwe as I was, back from receiving an award from the United Nations. He was up front in first class, of course, and I had a glimpse of him. Our disembarkation was delayed at the Harare airport while we waited for Mugabe to shake hands with the international diplomatic corps on the tarmac.

I attended planning and training sessions for EPI field workers and survey interviewers in the provincial town of Masvingo, about 300 kilometres south of Harare, the capital. I accompanied one survey team to rural villages and observed them conducting a cluster survey.

One of our survey sites was located on a white-owned commercial farm. It was very interesting to observe the interactions between Black and white Zimbabweans in this setting. The Black interviewers felt intimidated and were resentful, while the white farmers were outwardly cooperative but barely hiding their suspicion and condescension. In the late 1990s, Mugabe initiated a "land reform" by confiscating white-owned farms. Though much needed and intended to be redistributed to needy African farmers, many of the vacated farms went actually to enrich his political cronies in ZANU.

In the 1980s, CIDA contributed multi-year funding to UNICEF, part of which went to support India's universal immunization program. In 1989, I was part of a team of two consultants contracted by CIDA to conduct a program review and identify future needs and potential continuing support. We travelled across the country, from Delhi and Jaipur in the north, to Hyderabad in the centre, to Madras and Vellore in the south. I was able to see a little bit of the rich geographic, cultural, ethnic, and economic diversity of the country. Unfortunately, the social and caste disparities were all too obvious. We did the usual rounds of interviews with health officials at the Union, state, and district levels, professional organizations, NGOs, and training centres. We went to several frontline health centres and dispensaries. I observed how committed, overworked, and underpaid the frontline (female) nurses were. In the rural districts, they had to travel by overcrowded buses, carrying their medical kits, and jostle with throngs of passengers. Meanwhile, their bosses, the (male) district medical officers, zipped around the countryside in chauffeured UNICEF Land Rovers, ostensibly to supervise how the nurses worked.

A nurse teaching mothers about oral rehydration, near Hyderabad

I am not convinced that a consultant visit over a few weeks is very helpful for the donor to determine if their development aid is being used appropriately and effectively. I suppose this type of assessment constitutes "due diligence" for the auditors. Clearly, the ultimate evaluation of the effectiveness of an immunization program is to find out how much the coverage has increased and whether the rates of new cases of diseases have declined. This type of data can only be obtained over time and requires a functioning surveillance system.

From the 1990s on, I did not undertake any further overseas consultancy trips. My main interests had by then switched almost entirely to Northern and Indigenous health in Canada, although I maintained an ongoing interest in global health. My later international work was in the Arctic countries and countries with a significant Indigenous population, such as Australia, Brazil, and the United States.

I am ambivalent about international development assistance. The needs are clearly enormous and most of the people working in development agencies are dedicated and committed. Unfortunately, the effectiveness and impact of assistance projects are often hampered by systemic barriers and obstacles at both the donor and recipient ends. Donor countries may not always have altruistic motives, and often promote their own products and services in their projects. There may be strings attached in terms of political advantage for the donors, such as United Nations votes. Projects may not be what the recipient countries need or consider high priority. Recipient countries may become dependent on and even addicted to such assistance, which can, for instance, become needed to pay government workers' salaries. How much of the aid actually reaches those in need of it? Many recipient countries are notorious for their rampant corruption and wastefulness. I admit that I have no firm conclusions on this complex issue, other than that the world badly needs rich countries to assist in the economic and social development of poor countries.

This chapter was entitled "African Interlude," primarily to describe our time in Tanzania, though it also includes visits to Zimbabwe, the Philippines, and India, making it broadly a chapter about global health. It would not be out of place to mention my first visit to China, in 1978, on a four-week, ten-city package tour with a group of Chinese Canadians. I was then a graduate student at U of T, and seized the opportunity to fulfill a lifelong dream. I was able to leave the group toward the end of the tour to visit my uncle in Chengdu, Szechwan, where he was professor of occupational medicine.

Mao had died earlier, in 1976, and China was in transition. By then, the Gang of Four had already been dispatched and there was peace and quiet. I had never been to China before. Until that time, I had been a fervent admirer of the achievements of the People's Republic, which had transformed from an underdeveloped country subjugated by foreign imperialists into one that was proud and self-reliant. The Chinese people made sacrifices for the common good. While I was aware of the various man-made disasters—the Hundred Flowers Campaign, the Great Leap Forward, and the Cultural Revolution, to name a few—I swallowed the official justifications and denials of atrocities and sufferings. I was not alone, as in the West, people who did not have to live under the regime were generous with their praise.

With a barefoot doctor in a people's commune near Shanghai, 1978

We flew to Beijing from Tokyo on a CAAC flight (Civil Aviation Administration of China). The attendants wore plain white shirts and grey trousers with no makeup, a refreshing contrast to those working for Western airlines, and passengers were offered cigarettes along with snacks and drinks. Cigarettes were all-pervasive then, even considered an essential part of hospitality. I was quite emotional when the plane landed on Chinese soil.

As expected, our group was under the watchful eyes of our official escorts wherever we went. In the 1970s, there were few Western visitors, a far cry from today's glitzy five-star hotels and hordes of tourists. Of particular interest to me was a visit we made to a people's commune near Shanghai, where we met the barefoot doctor in charge. Barefoot doctors were China's answer to the community health workers that were being deployed widely across the developing world, not unlike the health aides in northern Canada. They were not literally barefoot—the name signified the humble peasant origins of those who worked for the benefit of their communities. They received only basic training, unlike the medical assistants in Tanzania who underwent a formal three-year program. As it turned out, the person I met at the commune clinic was the same person featured in a documentary film on health care in China made by Peter New of U of T. It seemed that this particular health worker and his clinic were trotted out whenever a foreign group wanted to see the barefoot doctors in action. Sadly, with the new economic policies introduced by Deng Xiaoping, barefoot doctors were phased out in the 1980s as the rural health care system became increasingly privatized.

At the end of the tour, I left my group and flew to Chengdu. There was a stopover in a small airfield in Kweiyang, where lunch was served. I was escorted to a room all by myself and ate alone, separated from the other passengers. It seemed that no effort was spared to keep tourists from having any contact with ordinary Chinese people. My being allowed to visit my uncle may have had something to do with his degree of redness, i.e. he was deemed reliable (for now) by the Party and unlikely to be compromised. It was the first time I met my uncle, the one who had been beaten by the Japanese during the Occupation. He had left Hong Kong immediately after the war and never returned. He was a die-hard supporter of the regime and a survivor. I never knew what kind of ups and downs he had experienced during the numerous campaigns and purges over the years. Being from Hong Kong was always a black mark that could one day, depending on who was in control, be brought against a person, requiring them to undergo self-criticism sessions or show trials.

While in Chengdu, I went on a bicycle ride into the city centre with my cousins and had the most hair-raising experience. Suddenly I was among thousands of cyclists, all experts, who cut in and out, jostling one another. Alas, I believe today any traffic jam in China is due to private cars rather than bicycles.

I had an unsettling experience on my last day in China. I was resting in my hotel room in Canton. A man came in unannounced, never introduced himself, and asked me what I thought of the New China. He said, "We have done some bad things over the years, but on the whole, it has been good. I am sure you have seen things that you may not like. As an overseas Chinese, it is your duty to help spread a positive image about China."

I have not been back to China since, other than one short visit with Valerie and our two boys to Canton in 1988 when we took the hydrofoil from Hong Kong, and I have no desire to do so.

The slogan reads: "Seize every minute and second, rush forward toward the year 2000"

6.

Academia Beckons

From Tanzania we returned to Sioux Lookout. After serving as medical director there from 1980 to 1983, I realized that a career in government was not for me. Deep down, I was an academic. Even early on in my career, I had tried to analyze and write about my experiences, such as the conflict between the citizen board and the physicians at the community clinic in Regina. In Sioux Lookout, I took advantage of the region's comprehensive medical records and conducted some descriptive epidemiological studies on tuberculosis, cancer, and causes of mortality. A single source of health care and comprehensive medical records in a geographically defined population definitely facilitated such studies.

Across the border in Winnipeg, there was a sister northern program at the University of Manitoba (U of M) called the Northern Medical Unit (NMU). It was developed and directed by Jack Hildes, associate dean of community medicine and a noted physiologist who had done ground-breaking research on human cold adaptation in the Arctic. I sought him out and visited him in Winnipeg to discuss an academic career, and he welcomed me warmly. I was also introduced to David Fish, head of the Department of Social and Preventive Medicine, later renamed Community Health

Sciences (CHS), who agreed to appoint me as an assistant professor. Unfortunately, by the time I began my appointment, Jack Hildes had been diagnosed with brain cancer, passing away shortly after. I never had the privilege of working with him. His successor, Brian Postl, took me under his wing instead, as did Michael Moffatt.

Starting my academic career in a place such as U of M was the right move. CHS offered me a supportive environment to pursue my research interests. Its involvement in health service delivery and research in northern Manitoba and the Keewatin region of the Northwest Territories (now part of Nunavut) was exactly what I had been looking for. I was among like-minded people. I stayed at U of M from 1983 to 2001 and rose through the ranks from assistant to full professor. Right from the very beginning, it was a clear expectation that I must earn my keep by obtaining research grants and career development awards, which I managed to do throughout my academic career.

Coming from a "weekend researcher" background in Sioux Lookout, I had to quickly learn the game of academic grantsmanship. I did not have a PhD then and was weak on methodology. My colleagues in CHS were high-powered researchers. In my first year, I gave a presentation to my departmental colleagues on a research proposal. It was an amateurish attempt, and my inadequacy was patently obvious. One junior colleague said that "there was blood on the floor" afterwards and felt sorry for me. While bad for my ego, the presentation was a wake-up call. I resolved to take advanced courses in epidemiology and biostatistics at summer schools in Minneapolis and Boston, and not to shy away from seeking advice and guidance from my seniors.

My very first successful grant was a modest one from the Children's Hospital of Winnipeg Foundation, to conduct a case-control study on the Bacillus Calmette-Guérin (BCG) vaccination among Indigenous newborns. There was quite a bit of controversy surrounding the effectiveness of the BCG vaccine against tuberculosis at the time. It was still widely used in developing countries but had largely been abandoned in developed ones. Indigenous children were among the few populations in Canada that still received the vaccine. My study entailed travelling across the province to visit nursing stations and review health records. The results—that the vaccine was at least sixty percent effective—were published in 1986 in the *American Journal of Public Health* and received widespread attention. They were even translated into Spanish and published in *Infectologia*, a Mexican journal.

In addition to teaching and research, I was also involved in an administrative capacity at the NMU. It had five service areas, each headed by a medical program coordinator. I was appointed as one such coordinator and assigned to the Island Lake cluster of four First Nations communities in northeastern Manitoba. My role was to act as a liaison between the communities and the federal government and supervise the GPs serving those communities. The tripartite university-community-government contractual relationship was extremely complex, and often rocky.

While the NMU was contracted by the federal government to provide physician services in various northern communities, the arrangement enabled it to conduct research on the side. I believed the time was ripe for a formal research unit within CHS, as there was already a core group of researchers whose main interests lay in northern and Indigenous health. In 1986, the Northern Health Research Unit was launched, and I served as its founding director until 1994. The unit grew over the years and underwent several transformations, first into the Centre for Aboriginal Heath Research in 2001 in partnership with the Assembly of Manitoba Chiefs, and into the faculty-wide Institute of Indigenous Health and Healing in 2017, consolidating various programs in education, research, and service. Thus, U of M continued to take the Canadian lead in Indigenous health. All the other university programs established in the 1970s, including U of T's Sioux Lookout Project, had fallen by the wayside.

I had always wanted to pursue a PhD. While physicians have long claimed that the MD is the "real" doctor, the word's Latin root actually means "teacher," and has nothing to do with healing. Though I already had a thesis-based MSc after my MD and had amply demonstrated that I could conduct research, I felt I needed further academic credentials, the highest of which was a PhD. Early in the 1990s, I began to look around for suitable places to obtain just that. Since I had three degrees from Canada, I thought that my next and last one should be from either the US or the UK. I considered epidemiology at the University of Minnesota, which was just across the border from Manitoba, but rejected that idea when their department head sent me back an impersonal letter and an application form in response to my inquiry. That left two other choices: epidemiology at the London School of Hygiene and Tropical Medicine, or biological anthropology at Oxford. I wrote to Geoffrey Rose at London and Geoffrey Ainsworth Harrison at Oxford, major figures in public health and anthropology respectively. Both wrote back personally and were extremely encouraging. In the summer of 1991, while visiting her parents in England, Valerie and I stopped in London and Oxford where I had warm meetings with Rose and Harrison. While in Oxford, we took a tour on top of an open double-decker bus. I was entranced. Right then and there, I decided that Oxford was my kind of place. I also thought that I should do something different from epidemiology, but not so different that it would require me to completely retool myself. Biological anthropology, which also contains a population perspective, fit the bill perfectly, especially since I had been doing field work for all those years in Indigenous communities in Canada. And so, in October 1992, I became a student again. My academic home was the Institute of Biological Anthropology, headed by Harrison. My college was Linacre, an exclusively graduate institution, enabling me to avoid undergraduates half my age.

In academic garb [sub fusc], Linacre College, 1992

I was able to plunge immediately into writing my thesis, based on analysis of the data collected from the Keewatin Health Assessment Study. The thesis was entitled *Human Obesity and Arctic Adaptation: Epidemiological Patterns, Metabolic Effects, and Evolutionary Implications*. I was awarded my PhD in 1995.

In 1998, I was appointed as head of the Department of Community Health Sciences at U of M. It was quite an honour and a privilege, as CHS was an outstanding department with a very strong research-intensive faculty and commitment to service for diverse communities. It had twenty-five full-time faculty members.

Its specialized research centres had achieved national and international recognition, especially the Manitoba Centre for Health Policy and Evaluation (MCHPE), under the leadership of Noralou Roos, and the Centre for Aboriginal Health Research, led by John O'Neil. Both were awarded the highly competitive Canada Foundation for Innovation grants to develop state-of-the-art research facilities. That CHS, considered part of the "soft" sciences, scored such huge hits ahead of the big boys in the basic sciences and clinical departments was particularly sweet. In education, CHS was involved in all levels—undergraduate medicine, thesis-based MSc and PhD programs, residencies in community medicine, postdoctoral fellowships, and programs for clinical scholars. Significantly, CHS coordinated access programs to support Indigenous students' entry into and progression through health professional training programs. The "community" in the CHS name was well deserved—the NMU served over twenty-five Indigenous communities in northern Manitoba and Nunavut, while MCHPE was awarded multi-year contracts from the provincial health ministry to conduct research utilizing health care databases to improve health system performance.

Not much management is involved in being department head or dean in a university. Budgets are fixed, if not actually declining, and while there is certainly room for hiring, firing is generally not possible. One needs to seize unforeseen opportunities and additional resources whenever they arise. I am not a fan of strategic planning, which amounts to vivid daydreaming. Unfortunately, countless person-hours are spent on it everywhere, and the plans remain largely unfulfilled. Academics also love to indulge in producing a mission statement, which consumes an inordinate amount of time and often induces conflict. My main role as an academic leader was to mentor students and junior faculty and to be on the lookout for opportunities that could enhance their prospects. A leader must protect and promote the interests of the academic unit—like pigs at the trough, department heads jostle for crumbs from the dean, and deans do likewise from the provost.

Academic organizations are diametrically opposed to the military. One cannot order a professor to do x, y, or z. All professors, regardless of rank, report to a single chair or head. Academic leaders must have strong credentials and understand the environment. Even business school deans are drawn from among academics, rather than from CEOs of corporations. In government, subject-matter expertise is not valued or considered necessary—a deputy minister can run Fisheries one day, and Health the next.

I served only three-and-a-half years of the five-year term as department head at U of M because U of T came calling. In Canada, U of T clearly occupies the top rung of the academic career ladder. I decided that eighteen years at U of M had been long enough, and there was still room for another move, another adjustment, another challenge. The U of T Department of Public Health Sciences, chaired by Harvey Skinner at the time, was the largest and most comprehensive research and training ground for public health in Canada. I was not entirely a stranger, as I had completed my MSc there back in the late 1970s, although all of my old professors had retired. There was another reason. My brother Julian was by then living in a nursing home in Toronto, and three of my sisters were also living in the area.

I said goodbye to U of M, and in January 2002, I started at U of T. Valerie and the boys stayed in Winnipeg so that she did not have to quit her job and the boys did not have to change schools. I bought a condo directly opposite Sunnybrook Park and used public transport to go to work, as I did not own a car. I flew back and forth between Toronto and Winnipeg, garnering a large number of frequent flyer points along the way, which were put to good use for my family's travels.

Harvey Skinner had a vision of transforming Public Health Sciences from a department within the Faculty of Medicine into a separate, free-standing School of Public Health. This only became a reality in 2013, when the new Dalla Lana School of Public Health was inaugurated. U of T had in fact had a School of Hygiene established back in 1927, among a handful of American and foreign schools funded by the Rockefeller Foundation. A francophone school at Université de Montréal was established in 1945. By the mid-1970s, however, both schools were defunct and had been absorbed into faculties of medicine. At that time, public health was deemed to be no longer relevant, what with the apparent conquest of infectious diseases and the great technological strides in curative medicine. However, the SARS epidemic in 2003 demonstrated how critical a sound public health system is. In 2020, with the COVID-19 pandemic, history appeared to have repeated itself.

With friend Peter Bjerregaard by lamp post, Hart House Circle, 2012

A year after my arrival, I was made acting chair of Public Health Sciences while Harvey Skinner went on sabbatical leave. I enjoyed being in that role, as it gave me insight into the inner workings of a major institution.

In 2002, the TransCanada Pipelines Corporation endowed a chair in Indigenous health at U of T, and its first holder was Jeff Reading, an Indigenous scientist. When he left the university in 2004, I was appointed in his place. The word "pipelines" was quietly dropped from the chair name when their construction became a controversial issue in academia and outside. Because the company's nationwide network of pipelines either passed through or near First Nations territories, its endowing a chair in Indigenous health was intended as a demonstration of corporate social responsibility. Other than its annual report on the great things the chairholder had done, the donor made little contact. In 2012, dean of medicine Catherine Whiteside and I went to the TransCanada corporate headquarters in Calgary, caps in hand, hoping to persuade them to contribute additional funds to the support of Indigenous health research and education. Alas, this effort was made in vain. U of T, however, did not hesitate to showcase its Indigenous health chair in its capital campaigns. During one such campaign, my portrait was hung on a lamppost on campus, among scores of other, more deserving luminaries.

Health research in Canada underwent a momentous change in 2002 when the Medical Research Council of Canada became the Canadian Institutes of Health Research (CIHR). The funding agency formally recognized that health research did not just mean biomedical research. Of its thirteen institutes, one was for population and public health and another for Indigenous people's health, along with others that were the more traditionally focused on body parts and diseases. I was appointed to the advisory board of the

Institute of Population and Public Health, whose scientific director was John Frank, the former CUSO cooperant whose job and house I had taken over in Tanzania some two decades earlier. Those were heady days, as we were able to plot the direction of public health research in Canada. Jeff Reading, former TransCanada chair at U of T, headed the sister institute on Indigenous people's health.

Academic life involves substantial extramural activities—serving on boards, committees, panels, task forces, and the like. While time consuming, most are interesting and informative, especially those that are somewhat outside one's area of expertise.

With men in the Xingu Indigenous Park, Brazil, 1991

Visiting professorships are highly sought after, especially international ones. In 1991, I was invited to the Escola Paulista de Medicina in São Paulo, Brazil, by Roberto Baruzzi, who had a lifelong interest in the health of Indigenous Amazonians. He developed a program of service delivery and research in the Xingu Indigenous Park, not unlike that of the Northern Medical Unit at U of M. In addition to rounds of seminars and public lectures, I was given the rare opportunity to accompany Baruzzi's team on their annual visit to Xingu Park, through which the Xingu River, a tributary of the Amazon, flows. At least in its English translation, the term "park" is unfortunate. It was established in 1961 to protect the environment and Indigenous people within it—both were threatened by encroaching mining, logging, and agribusiness developments. By the 1990s, when flying over the rainforests, one could see pockets of bush that had been burned and cleared as far as the eye could see. The Indigenous people had been only minimally affected by external influences. Most, young and old, still walked around naked, with their bodies painted with red ochre. They slept in hammocks in longhouses, and their diet consisted mainly of manioc (cassava) and fish. One extremely hot afternoon, during a break from the clinic, everybody went for a swim. Trying to blend in with our hosts, I took all my clothes off and dived in. When I surfaced, I saw that I was the only person among the visitors who was swimming *au naturel*. I count that as my most embarrassing moment. Indigenous people in the Xingu region are very different from the Indigenous people of North America in many ways, but one thing they have in common is their struggle to protect their culture, lands, and way of life. In fact, several of the Xingu tribal leaders subsequently became prominent advocates and defenders of their people's rights in the international arena.

In 2001, the Chinese University of Hong Kong nominated me for the SLL Wong Visiting Fellowship, which was awarded annually to a prominent scholar of Chinese heritage who would then deliver public lectures and meet students and faculty to promote academic and cultural interchanges. Among previous fellows was Yang Chen-ning, Nobel laureate in physics. I was clearly not in the same league, and I did not think academics in Hong Kong were even interested in my work in Indigenous health. However, I was pleasantly surprised by the high degree of interest, especially among students. I was impressed by this new generation, and my interactions with them reassured me that there was a future for Hong Kong—later clearly demonstrated by their commitment to freedom and willingness to stand up to tyranny. I was feted to a degree that no Canadian university that I was aware of ever bestowed on a visitor. There was even a huge banner across the campus entrance reading "Welcome Professor Kue Young" in bright red Chinese characters. I was interviewed by a reporter for a Chinese-language newspaper, and the next day there was a full-page article about my unusual career path, at least for someone from Hong Kong.

While at U of M, I was appointed by the provincial government to the Manitoba Human Rights Commission. It was an interesting experience. We met once a month and spent a day or two reviewing and adjudicating cases of complaints and charges of violation of human rights legislations. The cases were mostly employment related. For example, we were once asked to decide on whether the city's recreation department could specify the gender in a job vacancy advertisement for a cleaner in the changing rooms of municipal swimming pools. A long debate ensued as to whether a woman cleaner had the right to clean the men's changing room full of swimmers in different stages of undress, or vice versa. When the world is full of genocides, ethnic cleansing, and torture, our human rights issues surely paled in comparison. In the Canadian context, I am not denigrating these human rights issues, which clearly still must be redressed.

With its transformation of the health research environment, CIHR launched many new strategic initiatives that were cross-disciplinary and jointly funded by several institutes. Among these were multi-year, multi-million-dollar grants to establish large teams. I received one such grant while at U of M, focused on diabetes in the Indigenous population. Ten projects were launched under five themes: assessing disease burden, identifying risk factors, discovering metabolic pathways, understanding cultural knowledge, and designing and implementing interventions. Even while I was at Sioux Lookout in the 1980s, diabetes was beginning to be recognized as an emerging health problem. After starting my research career at U of M, I decided to focus on chronic diseases, including diabetes, within Indigenous populations. I continued to be preoccupied with this subject for the next three decades.

Another important initiative, this one funded by CIHR's Institute of Indigenous People's Health under the leadership of Jeff Reading, aimed to expand research capacity through training support and infrastructure development. I was awarded one such grant for a project that spanned eight years. In partnership with researchers at several Ontario universities and with Indigenous communities and organizations, we were able to develop the Indigenous Health Research Program (IHRDP) based at U of T, and the Six Nations Polytechnic in Ohsweken, Ontario. In that time, we were able to grant graduate scholarships and research allowances to some fifty students at the master's, doctoral, and postdoctoral levels. Many of the award recipients went on to become full-fledged academic researchers sprinkled across the country, forming the core of an emerging community of Indigenous researchers.

A summer institute in session for IHRDP trainees

We also provided small seed grants to enable Indigenous communities and organizations to develop, plan, and implement research projects that they had identified as their priority. There was a special category of Indigenous knowledge awards to engage elders and knowledge keepers in research projects.

At U of T, a formal Collaborative Program in Aboriginal Health was developed. It offered courses and seminars to students from various graduate programs in the health sciences, social sciences, and education, completion of which enabled them to add Aboriginal Health as a specialization to their degrees. Every summer, we organized seasonal institutes that addressed current issues relevant to Indigenous health research and offered intensive workshops on special topics, such as research ethics and scientific publishing.

Ideally, toward the end of one's career, accolades begin to pour in. I am very proud of the fact that in 2009 I was inducted as Fellow of the Canadian Academy of Health Sciences and, a year later, was made a Member of the Order of Canada. More than anything else, these honours validated my work over the course of my career.

With David Johnston, Governor-General of Canada, 2011

I stayed at U of T for twelve years, but eventually got itchy feet again. While I enjoyed research, I felt less and less excited about getting yet another grant and publishing yet another paper. My stints as department head gave me a sense of what being an academic administrator was like, and I thought I could go one step further.

In 2006, the University of Alberta (U of A) was the first among Canadian universities to establish a free-standing School of Public Health. A few years later, the Universities of Saskatchewan, Toronto, and Montréal followed suit. A former provincial deputy minister of health served as interim dean while a search for the first dean was underway. Becoming the dean of a school of public health appealed to me greatly, a position in which one would play a critical leadership role in the public health profession in Canada. I applied, but made it only to the final shortlist consisting of me and one other candidate. In the end, they offered the job to a former senior public health officer in the federal government. So that was that, and I put my ambition aside.

As it turned out, that dean lasted only two years. For a variety of reasons, her term was cut short by the provost. I personally believed that a high office in government did not prepare one well for academic administration, but then, I was obviously biased. In any case, the search was on again. The provost—not the one who had turned me down earlier—phoned me up and asked if I would be interested. Of course I was interested, but I did not think my ego could stand a second rejection. While they had to follow due process, they were clearly very keen on me. Early in 2013, I visited the U of A campus in Edmonton, a city I had only set foot in twice before in all my years in Canada. I went through the same routine of interviews, a public presentation, and sumptuous dinners with the search committee, presumably to check out if I was sound. In the end, I was selected. In August 2013, I embarked on the final stage of my career, as dean of the School of Public Health.

I began my deanship shortly after my sixty-fifth birthday. I formally retired from U of T and was appointed professor emeritus. By that time, Valerie had already retired from her dental practice in Winnipeg. We had bought a house in Fernie, British Columbia, which was to be our retirement home. While Valerie moved, I continued my commuting existence, now a much shorter one between Edmonton and Fernie. In Edmonton, I rented an apartment within walking distance from campus.

During her time in Winnipeg, Valerie first worked for an outreach program of the U of M Dental Faculty, visiting long-term care homes to provide much-needed services to the residents. She then worked at the Mount Carmel Clinic, long known as a community clinic serving initially Jewish immigrants and refugees from Europe. Later, the clinic served citizens of the inner city of Winnipeg, low-income people with no dental insurance, often underserved and marginalized. She also worked on the City of Winnipeg's dental program serving inner city school children.

Ideally, when looking for a post-retirement job, one wants to be paid a handsome salary without having to do much work. While a dean's salary was indeed substantial, it was a difficult (but enjoyable) job. I did have some trepidation—would I be living proof of the Peter principle, promoted to the level of incompetence? One thing I did make clear to my superiors and colleagues was that I fully intended to serve only one five-year term and retire in 2018, when I would be seventy years old.

The School of Public Health (SPH) was small, with thirty-five full-time faculty members and around 300 students pursuing the MSc, MPH, and PhD degrees. In 2012, SPH had been awarded accreditation for five years by the US-based Council on Education in Public Health. In my final year, my colleagues and I worked hard to achieve, successfully, a renewal of that accreditation, this time for seven years. Until then, U of A and Université de Montréal were the only accredited Canadian schools. U of T had decided that accreditation was not needed.

I learned something new as dean—curling at our annual bonspiel for students, staff and faculty

In its short history, SPH has demonstrated its academic excellence, productivity, and innovation, despite its small size. Its research revenue has been exceeded only by the much larger faculties of engineering, science, medicine, and agriculture. It attracted students from across Canada and beyond. Its Centre for Healthy Communities focused on the built environment. The executive Fellowship Program in Health System Improvement has instilled a population and systems perspective in several cohorts of health care leaders from across the country. Towards the end of my term, I began several initiatives to develop and strengthen northern and Indigenous health at the school.

I was fortunate to have Faith Davis as my vice-dean, an internationally-known cancer epidemiologist who had returned to her home province after many years in the United States, loaded with advanced degrees from Harvard and Yale, and years of experience at the University of Illinois in Chicago. The environment at SPH was certainly very collegial. I considered myself approachable, and had an open-door policy for faculty and students alike.

An unavoidable downside of academic administration was the innumerable number of meetings one needed to attend. It did not take long for me to ascertain which ones were important and which were mere talking shops. When gathered around the table, deans and assorted vice-presidents preened themselves and tried to outdo each other in one-upmanship. Everybody wanted to have their say, even if they were repeating something that had already been said. Nevertheless, such forums were important to a small faculty such as SPH. For the school to avoid being regarded as an academic Cinderella, the dean needed to be assertive and constantly promoting its capabilities both internally and externally.

Early in December 2016, I joined a delegation to Iraqi Kurdistan, organized by University of Alberta International, intended to help develop a brand-new university with private funding. Our hosts expressed particular interest in two faculties: agriculture and public health.

The homeland of the Kurds stretches across Iran, Iraq, Syria, and Turkey, where they are not only unwelcome but persecuted. A nation of their own has long been a dream of theirs. The establishment of a no-fly zone over northern Iraq during the Gulf War enabled the Kurds to breathe easier, slowly develop their autonomous government structures, and avoid the sectarian violence endemic in the rest of Iraq.

The U of A delegation receives a warm welcome

We arrived in Irbil, the regional capital, on a direct flight from Frankfurt, to a warm welcome. We visited government ministries (and met the Prime Minister of the regional government), NGOs, and universities. We also traveled to the city of Sulaymaniyah in the east. The Kurds are secular Muslims and contain a large Christian minority. Christmas lights were already ablaze in the Christian sector. I was struck by the sight of huge billboards advertising Heineken beer. Kurdistan was an oasis of relative peace amidst the turmoil and instability in the rest of Iraq, despite the fact that Kurdish fighters (*pershmergas*) were heroically battling the Islamic State (*Daesh*) not far from the city. Security was tight everywhere, but not intrusively so. Impoverished to begin with, the Kurds had suffered decades of wars and strife. The war against the Islamic State generated thousands of refugees, whom the Kurds generously housed and fed, adding to their own economic woes. I worry that history will repeat itself, and that one day the Kurds will be betrayed and abandoned by their fair-weather friends.

Meeting with the Prime Minister of the Kurdistan Regional Government

In a museum inside the ancient citadel of Irbil, there was a rock that made me want to weep. The accompanying note explained, "This is just an ordinary rock, but it was there in Halabja in 1988 when Saddam Hussein massacred thousands of Kurds using chemical weapons." What a poignant silent witness to the atrocity. To many Kurds, the foreign invasion of Iraq that overthrew Saddam Hussein in 2003 was a just war.

U of A terminated the planning of the Kurdistan project to avoid a potential reputational risk when it came to light that the Iraqi consortium behind the initiative was under a cloud of financial irregularities. After our site visit, our enthusiasm for a private university in Kurdistan waned. We saw how public, government-run and -financed universities struggled under severe shortages of both human and financial resources. We should have been helping them instead of those who wanted to create a private for-profit university.

In reviewing my academic career, one may have gained the

impression that it was all a straight rise to the top. Not quite. I was passed over for department headships at both Manitoba and Toronto, although in the end I did eventually become department head at U of M. I have already mentioned that U of A rejected me the first time around. All's well that ends well. I had other successes. In the early 1990s, I was offered the position of head of community health at Memorial University of Newfoundland. I declined the offer, as I considered Newfoundland somewhat of an outlier both geographically and academically.

In 1996, I applied to the Aga Khan University (AKU) in Karachi for the position of head of community health. AKU is a private, English-language medical school, part of the Aga Khan's global network of charitable foundations and institutions. It had a very good reputation internationally. The dean of medicine at AKU was a former dean of the University of British Columbia, and we met at the Vancouver airport for an informal interview. I must have impressed him, because I was then invited to a personal interview in Karachi. It was my first-ever visit to a Muslim country. The department was very strong, with an excellent research record. I visited some of their field projects among fishermen, the rural poor, and urban women. The young faculty were very committed, and their attempts to improve the health of the marginalized and oppressed was indeed significant and meaningful. This heart-warming experience, however, was not sufficient to convince me that I would enjoy living and working in Karachi. They showed me some seaside houses designed for expatriates and owned by high-ranking army officers. What opulence! But could I live there amidst the squalor and deprivation of the rest of the city? Furthermore, the already precarious political situation was deteriorating—indeed, within a couple of years, in 1999, a military coup overthrew the civilian government. I was glad that I had not accepted the offer. AKU trained and produced physicians to a standard that was comparable to the best that the West had to offer, but I later read that, upon graduation, almost the entire class emigrated westward.

Covers of my seven books

Writing is very much a part of academic life. One's productivity is often judged by the quantity and quality of one's publications. I have always enjoyed writing, ever since my secondary school days, and it had been very much encouraged by my siblings. In Hong Kong, I wrote short pieces in English for a youth magazine and the children's corner of a Sunday newspaper. Later I even published two articles in Chinese, describing my experience in northern Canada and in Tanzania. These I sent to my brother Julian in Hong Kong for him to polish up and help get published in weekly magazines, where some high school classmates with whom I had long lost contact recognized my name. Since coming to Canada, my

Chinese writing skills had rapidly deteriorated. I did not read the Hong Kong newspapers that were easily available in Chinatowns. The only time I wrote in Chinese was to my mother. Even then, I had to look up words in the dictionary. Alas, that stopped when she passed away.

While I have written 170-odd journal articles over the course of my career, it is my seven books that are my pride and joy. As with everything else in life, the first one was the hardest to get published. *Health Care and Cultural Change* was published by the University of Toronto Press (UTP) in 1988, largely based on my MSc thesis of 1979. I learned that plonking a complete manuscript on the editor's desk—a practice referred to in the trade as "over the transom"—would definitely not work. Looking like a thesis would be a manuscript's kiss of death. UTP was initially not interested in my MSc thesis as book. I then tried about five different US and Canadian academic publishers and was rejected by all. In the end, I went back to UTP but tried a different tack. I prepared a book proposal with sample chapters, with the promise of a timely completion of the rest. They took the bait and I got my first-ever book contract. Later, with one book already published, it became easier to persuade an acquisitions editor. Of my seven books, four were by UTP, two by Oxford University Press, and one by Munksgaard, an international publisher based in Copenhagen. With the exception of a textbook titled *Population Health: Concepts and Methods*, all dealt with Indigenous and circumpolar health. My last book, *Circumpolar Health Atlas*, was truly beautiful. It was even awarded second place at the International Cartographic Exhibition in Dresden in 2013.

7.

Circumpolar Journeys

I ventured North of 60 for the first time in 1982, North of 60 being the term often used to refer to the northern territories of Canada collectively. I shall not attempt to define what constitutes the North, as much has already been written on the issue. I have adopted an operational definition; namely that the North, whether in Canada or elsewhere, consists of an agreed-upon list of administrative and political regions. It is in such regions where health data is generated and from where it is reported. Not all northern regions are in the Arctic, if Arctic is defined climatically.

In June 1982, I attended the annual conference of the Canadian Public Health Association held in Yellowknife, Northwest Territories (NWT). Sioux Lookout may be north in relation to Toronto, but it is located at 50° N, a mere stone's throw from the United States border. In Yellowknife, I experienced the midnight sun for the first time. I was to revisit that city many times.

Through the Northern Medical Unit at U of M, I had the opportunity to visit Churchill, Manitoba, and several Inuit communities farther north. In 1984, Brian Postl led a contingent of NMU staff and students to the International Conference on Circumpolar Health (ICCH) in Anchorage, Alaska. Thus began my long association with the ICCH. The congress (as the conference was now called) was held once every three years, rotating among circumpolar countries. The last congress I attended was in Copenhagen in 2018. There were ten congresses between those of Anchorage and Copenhagen, and I attended them all. It was very encouraging to see a crop of new and junior researchers and practitioners at each congress, while the core old-timers just kept coming back. The circumpolar health community will endure.

In 1985, I was awarded a WHO Travelling Fellowship. Most applicants applied to go south, whereas I went in the opposite direction to investigate the epidemiology and control of chronic diseases in Alaska and Greenland. I started in Anchorage and visited the Alaska Native Medical Center, the tertiary care referral hospital for Alaska Natives. From there I rented a car and drove to Fairbanks in the interior. I also flew to Bethel, a predominantly Yup'ik town at the mouth of the Yukon River, where there was a regional hospital. I interviewed practitioners, administrators, and researchers, and observed health care delivery firsthand. In the 1980s, it was becoming evident that Indigenous communities were undergoing rapid social changes, accompanied by changes in patterns of health and disease. The transition from the prevalence of infectious diseases to chronic diseases such as diabetes and heart disease was increasingly recognized across the Arctic. My travelling fellowship initiated international collaborations that later developed into joint health monitoring and health promotion projects.

My trip to Greenland was routed through Copenhagen, not the most direct or inexpensive route but one that was typical of their colonial relationship. Similarly, to go from East Africa to West Africa, one first had to fly north to London before going back south. Nevertheless, the stopover in Copenhagen was not wasted—much research on the health of Greenlanders was conducted by

Danes in Denmark who had spent some time in Greenland. I was introduced to Peter Bjerregaard, then a young researcher. His career path was very similar to mine—he had been a GP in Upernavik in northern Greenland, done a stint in Kenya working on an immunization program, and ended up in research. He had also started a mortality database for Greenland, which was constantly updated. When we first met, he was working at the Danish Institute of Clinical Epidemiology, later renamed the National Institute of Public Health, where he carved out a section on Greenland health research and built up quite a following of trainees and staff. He was later appointed Professor of Arctic Health. He conducted important research during his long association with Greenland, including several waves of a comprehensive health survey. We began a long and fruitful collaboration and friendship that continued for decades. Together we have co-authored fifteen papers and one book, and co-edited two other books. Though I have long been proclaiming that I have published my last paper on circumpolar health, that claim has been revised several times.

Icebergs in Disko Bay, near Ilulissat, Greenland

While in Greenland, I tagged along with the deputy chief medical officer and his dog on trips to the outlying towns and villages. We travelled by boat, as all settlements are coastal and not connected by road. The boat plied up and down the west coast of Greenland. I never did visit eastern Greenland, which is considerably more remote, even though it is quite close to Iceland geographically. In the 1980s, it appeared that most Danes smoked and drank to excess. Being cooped up in a small boat with everyone smoking and drinking, and the waves tossing us around, was not a pleasant experience. I was to return to Greenland on several other occasions to attend meetings in Ilulissat and Nuuk.

Graffiti on wall calling for democracy, Anadyr, Russia, 1989

I was able to visit the Soviet North thanks to Mikhail Gorbachev's policies of *glasnost* and *perestroika*, which opened up the country to foreign visitors. In 1988, the Medical Services Branch of Health and Welfare Canada signed a memorandum of understanding with the Siberian Branch of the USSR Academy of Medical Sciences to promote scientific exchanges and research collaboration between the two countries. This was the outcome of contacts made by senior Health and Welfare Canada officials with Russian delegates to the circumpolar health conference in Umeå, Sweden, in 1987. My colleague John O'Neil at U of M was instrumental in lobbying for the Northern Health Research Unit to be the lead agency for Canada. Our counterpart was the Academy's Institute of Internal Medicine in Novosibirsk, directed by Academician Yuri Nikitin. Two health surveys that focused on chronic diseases using similar protocols were conducted concurrently in the Keewatin region of NWT and the Chukotka Autonomous Okrug in the Soviet Union. The Keewatin Health Assessment Study was launched in 1990 with funding from Health and Welfare Canada. There were reciprocal site visits by the two teams as the projects progressed.

Chukchi dancers welcome Canadian visitors, Anadyr, 1989

In May 1989, a six-person delegation visited the Soviet Far East and Far North, comprising of John O'Neil, Mike Moffatt, and myself from U of M, Rosie Oolooyuk of the Keewatin Regional Health Board, Gill Lynch of Health and Welfare Canada, and

Ian Gilchrist of NWT Health and Social Services. We flew from Japan into Khabarovsk in the Soviet Far East, and from there to Magadan, Anadyr, and the two small Indigenous villages of New Chaplino and Provideniya. It was Rosie's first-ever trip outside Canada. We arrived at the Tokyo train station just as the bullet train arrived, disgorging thousands of passengers all at once. Rosie was astounded: "I have never seen so many people in one place. God has given each one of them a purpose." While in the Soviet Union, we visited medical institutes, research centres, polyclinics, and various cultural points of interest. The two predominant Indigenous groups are Chukchi and Siberian Yup'ik, related to the Yup'ik people in Alaska. I could now claim to have stood on both sides of the Bering Strait. Although Rosie's Inuktitut from the Central Arctic was not mutually intelligible with Siberian Yup'ik, she easily established bonds with the local people, who in turn were delighted to have met one of their kin from afar.

The trip ended on a bit of a sour note. All six of us passed through immigration and customs at Vancouver Airport together, but only Rosie Oolooyuk and I—the two non-whites—were pulled aside for questioning and had our baggage searched. One of our team members was visibly angry—"I have never been so ashamed of being a Canadian," he said.

The collaboration between health branches in Canada and Siberia operated on the principle of *bez valuta*, where no money actually changed hands or crossed borders. Essentially, the Russians paid for everything on Russian soil (including costs incurred by their own research project and the in-country travel of the foreign visitors) and the Canadians did likewise in Canada. Needless to say, we were treated like VIPs. We actually developed friendships with some of the researchers that outlasted the collaboration agreement. Overall, they were very knowledgeable and able to keep somewhat abreast of developments in the West, despite having access to a dearth of foreign journals.

If the colour grey characterized much of Soviet urban landscape—monuments and workers' apartments alike—it was even bleaker in the Arctic. The Soviet approach to northern development consisted of urbanization, industrialization, and collectivization. The oppression of Indigenous peoples and their cultures was only exposed to the outside world after the collapse of the USSR.

In May and June of 1991, Mike Moffatt and I traveled to Novosibirsk and gave presentations on the preliminary results of the Keewatin Study to our collaborators in the Academy. On our return via Moscow, we had a few hours before our departure and decided to do some sightseeing. To our horror, Mike discovered that he no longer had his passport and return ticket on him. We were frantic, and I was momentarily faced with a moral dilemma—should I leave Mike behind to fend for himself, or should I stay with him and help navigate our exit strategy? We rushed back to our hotel and up to our rooms, but we had checked out earlier and nothing could be found. To our relief, the babushka manning the floor—a regular feature of Soviet hotels who kept an eye on all the comings and goings—had Mike's precious cargo in hand. Because of this diversion, we missed our tour of the Kremlin but were happily on our way home regardless. When the pilot on our British Airways flight announced, "We have now left Soviet airspace," the passengers burst into spontaneous applause.

Unbeknownst to us visitors, momentous events were happening right under our noses. A couple of months later, in August, there was an attempted coup against Gorbachev, and in December, the once-mighty USSR disintegrated. The collapse of the old system seriously threatened scientific research. Funding previously allocated by the state evaporated and staff were let go *en masse*. Back at U of M, we read about the plight of our former collaborators. We collected a few hundred US dollars, put the bank notes inside a book, and mailed it to one of the young researchers whom we knew very well on a personal level—he had earlier visited my home in Winnipeg. Years later, we met again in one of the circumpolar conferences and he expressed his deep gratitude. A survivor, he had left the institute and gone into the pharmaceutical business.

The triennial ICCH was organized by the International Union for Circumpolar Health (IUCH), a federation of organizations from Canada, the United States, Russia, and the Nordic countries. I was elected the union's president from 1993 to 1996. It was a period of transition, when the congresses and the organization itself shifted their focus from the physiology of cold adaptation to public and Indigenous health.

The issue of designated representation for Indigenous people in the IUCH council came up during my term. It required two special meetings to reach a consensus after considerable debate. Typically, the Nordic countries were represented by senior physicians and professors who did not particularly see the need for such a provision. In Scandinavia, the 1960s and 1970s witnessed an awakening of Sami activism and struggle for political rights. Ester Fjellheim, a Norwegian Sami environmental activist, was a particularly vocal advocate of the council's need for reserved seats for Indigenous members. She was supported by the Canadian and Alaskan delegates. In the end, the IUCH statues were revised to stipulate that there must be at least one Indigenous person on the council. Over the years, the increasing prominence of Indigenous scientists and health professionals in circumpolar health meant that the requirement was easily fulfilled. Many distinguished Indigenous people played an active role in the IUCH. Among them were Ted Mala, an Alaska Native physician who later served as Health Commissioner for the State of Alaska; Jean Goodwill, a pioneer Cree nursing leader who was president of the Canadian Indigenous Nurses Association; and Bill Erasmus, Dene National Chief from the NWT.

Working with colleagues from the various national organizations of the IUCH provided me with the opportunity to be exposed to their very different scientific, academic, and political cultures. The Soviet Union had been represented by officials from the government-controlled Union of Medical Workers based in Moscow. It was not until after the dissolution of the USSR that individual scientists from Siberia were able to attend our conferences. In the 1990s, Alaska spearheaded exchanges with academic and health care institutions in Siberia. In 1992, I attended an Indigenous health conference in Wasila, Alaska, where Indigenous Russian health professionals were invited speakers. I was particularly impressed and touched by the testimony of Chukchi physician Larissa Abruytina, who detailed how they had suffered under decades of state-sponsored suppression of their languages and cultures, and how they were now able to become politically assertive and organized. Larissa was later elected as a member of the Duma, the national assembly of the Russian Federation.

In between congresses and beyond, the glue that kept the Union's members connected was the *International Journal of Circumpolar Health* (*IJCH*). The journal had a venerable history, dating back to 1973 when it was the organ of the Nordiska Samarbetskommitten för Artisk Medicinsk Forskning and called *Arctic Medical Research*. With the move of the editorial office to the Centre for Arctic Medicine at the University of Oulu, Finland, in 1997, the journal's name was changed to the present *IJCH*. To put it on a firmer financial footing, then editor-in-chief Juhani Hassi convinced several universities, research institutes, and professional and academic organizations to contribute to core funding on an annual basis. Over time, the interests of these participating institutions waxed and waned and the journal's finances remained precarious. Nevertheless, it managed to keep pace with the changing scientific publishing environment—going completely online in 2012; contracting a private publishing house to undertake editing, production, and promotion functions; and charging authors publication fees in 2013. I took over the editor-in-chief position in 2012 from Tiina Ikäheimo of Oulu, before stepping down in 2015 and handing over the reins to Rhonda Johnson of Anchorage. An important role of journals such as the *IJCH* was to provide a venue for junior, emerging researchers to present their ideas and test the waters. The hardest job of an editor was finding peer reviewers. Often, it was difficult to find *any* reviewers, let alone the *right* reviewers, who were subject-matter experts with a generous spirit, prompt in response, did not nitpick, and were not prone to trashing papers that they found unworthy.

Through our work on the journal, I got to know my Finnish friends Juhani Hassi and Tiina Ikäheimo quite well. Juhani invited us to his cottage in northern Lapland in 2004 and we witnessed the autumn changing of the colours (called *ruska* by the Finns) of the vegetation on the Arctic floor. Juhani managed to lead us on an eight-hour hike—our bodies and spirits were only resuscitated that evening by a sauna and a plunge into the lake.

The international aspects of circumpolar health are what make the field so interesting. Circumpolar countries include some with the most advanced and developed economies in the world, and yet considerable disparities exist within these countries between north and south, and between Indigenous and non-Indigenous people, although such disparities are by no means the same across all countries. The Sami in Scandinavia, especially Sami women, were better educated and had better health status than the average non-Sami. Despite the many differences in political systems, social policies, and health care, we can learn a lot from one another, sharing information on what works and what does not.

In 1996, the Arctic Council was created. Its members included the United States, Canada, Iceland, the Kingdom of Denmark with its autonomous territories of Greenland and the Faroe Islands, Norway, Sweden, Finland, and the Russian Federation. Foreign ministers of these countries met annually, and, once in a while, a treaty was signed on some aspect of circumpolar cooperation that everybody could live with. Significantly, the Council also invited organizations representing Indigenous peoples, especially those whose homelands crossed national borders. They were called Permanent Participants and they took part fully in the Council's deliberations. Issues of particular concerns to Arctic Indigenous peoples included the environment, natural resource development, the preservation and promotion of language and culture, and health.

In 2009, the Arctic Council created the Arctic Human Health Expert Group to provide advice on a variety of health issues. It met for the first time at the circumpolar health congress in Yellowknife. Peter Bjerregaard and I were the inaugural co-chairs. We served two three-year terms, during which time a few projects were completed, including workshops on suicide prevention and food security, the development of a circumpolar surveillance system for infectious diseases and the Circumpolar Health Observatory, comparative reviews of health systems, and a comparison of national and regional dietary guidelines. In 2011, health ministers of the Arctic countries convened at a summit in Nuuk and issued the Arctic Health Declaration to promote and affirm cooperation in health matters. Peter and I worked on a draft and submitted it to the Danish/Greenlandic chair. As expected, the final version that was formally signed bore little resemblance to our original draft, having gone through multiple layers of edits by diplomatic and political functionaries from different countries. Nevertheless, it was an interesting exercise.

I had the chance to return to Chukotka in December 1994 and

compare the region in the post-Soviet era with its former self from when we had last visited in 1989. The Circumpolar Affairs Directorate of the Department of Indian and Northern Affairs organized a mission to visit Arctic Russia. I was invited to the delegation as president of the IUCH. We were encouraged to develop a proposal for a project to support mobile medical teams serving remote communities. We submitted it to Foreign Affairs Canada for potential funding but were ultimately unsuccessful. With the economic collapse, Indigenous people in the Russian Arctic suffered disproportionately in terms of poor health and social deprivation. In Chukotka, many of the state-owned collective farms and reindeer herding brigades went bankrupt. Health care was gutted when the withdrawal of state support for remote regions led to massive out-migration of non-Indigenous settlers, among them health care workers. Even so, the Russian North continued to be oversupplied with physicians and hospital beds compared to other circumpolar regions.

The billowing smokestacks of Egvekinot and the air laden with soot produced a "darkness at noon"

The 1994 visit provided a glimpse of post-Soviet life in the two Arctic communities of Anadyr and Egvekinot. While the superficial changes were easily detectable to the casual observer, such as the availability of a wide variety of expensive imported foods and goods and the style and content of television programs, harder to gauge was the people's adaptation to the changing economic, social, and political environments. I detected an ambivalence towards the long-cherished but now discredited Soviet ideology, yet the still poorly-defined new order was fraught with uncertainties. Individuals and institutions were unsure of what to reject and retain from the old system, and what to import and adopt in terms of ideas, concepts and practices. While there was palpable relaxation in people's attitudes and outlook, old bureaucratic habits die hard, and the average Russian citizen continued to suffer and endure the deadening hand of indifferent, incompetent, and incomprehensible officialdom.

Chukotka in the dead of the Arctic winter brought home the brutal *gulag* past of the region. In Anadyr, the only bits of colour on the grey walls of the rows of dilapidated apartment blocks—remnants of socialist realist mural art—had faded.

I met many wonderful people in my circumpolar journeys and projects. I have already mentioned Peter Bjerregaard of Denmark and Greenland. In Canada, the grand old man was Otto Schaefer, a German physician who immigrated to Canada in the early 1950s to realize his dream of working among the Inuit in the Arctic. In 1964, he had been appointed founding director of the Northern Medical Research Unit of Health and Welfare Canada based in Edmonton. His research interests were wide-ranging, including infectious diseases, cancer, diabetes, nutrition, and respiratory diseases. He subscribed to a broad view of health, and had long championed the importance of sociocultural factors in shaping the health of northern communities undergoing rapid changes. We first met at a conference sometime in the 1980s and struck up a correspondence, with periodic encounters at meetings. His letters were typed single-spaced and double-sided, with handwritten supplementary notes in the margins that ran around the page. Someone once said of Otto that he spoke five languages, all of them German. After his retirement, he retreated to his mountain home in Jasper, Alberta. He died in 2009 at the age of ninety, much mourned and missed by those who had known, respected, and loved this gentle man with the charming accent. The medical library at the U of A maintains the Otto Schaefer Archives, containing the manuscripts, photos, and memorabilia that reflect a mere fraction of his encyclopedic knowledge of all things Arctic.

Another distinguished Canadian northern scientist was Éric Dewailly. Originally from Lille, France, he spent much of his academic career in Canada, mainly at Université Laval in Québec. Trained as a physician, epidemiologist, and toxicologist, he made major contributions to the study of environmental contaminants among the Inuit in the Nunavik region of Québec. He also made sure that his research was translated into public health policy and practice by working closely with the regional health board. Éric was fond of organizing Arctic health meetings in tropical locales such as Bermuda. When I told him I might have trouble getting my travel approved, he shook his head and complained about English Canadian puritanism. Tragically, Éric died a very premature death at the age of fifty-seven in 2014. While holidaying with his family on the Indian Ocean island of Réunion, he was killed by a rockslide. The large cadre of his former trainees and the body of scientific knowledge he produced were his legacy. No greater tribute was made than the one by Minnie Grey, executive director of the

Nunavik Regional Health Board, who expressed what we all felt: "Éric was a generous, kind, and inspirational man, always available for the Inuit, and his tremendous work helped us in a way that words cannot fully express. His unique knowledge, his love for the North, and his presence will be greatly missed by all."

In 2004, Éric was able to secure funding, primarily from the Québec provincial government and ArcticNet, and launched a comprehensive health survey in the Nunavik communities in northern Québec. ArcticNet was one of the Networks of Centres of Excellence funded by the Canadian government. While focused mainly on the physical sciences, it had some spare change left over for health research. Of particular importance was the refurbishing of the Coast Guard icebreaker *Amundsen* into a research vessel. Éric's Nunavik survey was carried out on the *Amundsen*, and participants were invited on board to be interviewed, examined, and tested. Peter was a passenger and an observer, and, shortly after, he launched his own parallel shipborne survey in Greenland with Danish funding, though without the benefit of the *Amundsen*.

Polar bears on the sea ice, seen from the deck of the *Amundsen*

That left the whole of northern Canada yet to be surveyed. Fortunately, the International Polar Year (IPY) arrived just in time. Held once every fifty years, the fourth IPY was scheduled for 2007 and 2008. The Canadian government earmarked over 150 million dollars in research funding. Unlike previous IPYs, this time attention was paid to human issues such as health, and not just sea ice, permafrost, and polar bears. McGill University's Centre for Indigenous Health and Nutrition had just recruited Grace Egeland, an American epidemiologist from Alaska, as a Canada Research Chair. Grace took the lead in preparing the proposal to the IPY Secretariat for funding, and we spent a couple of years travelling across the NWT, Nunavut, and Labrador to generate support from Inuit communities and regional governments.

Inuit Health Survey poster and map

The Inuit Health Survey was conducted during the two summers of 2007 and 2008, and covered all Inuit communities in the NWT,

Nunavut, and Labrador. I joined the team for part of the voyage during the second summer. Sailing on the icebreaker across the Arctic from Tuktoyaktuk to Resolute Bay was a journey of a lifetime. Beyond the stark beauty of the land and sea, one also sensed the fragility of the Arctic. One day, the whole ship was agog when a mother polar bear and her cub were sighted on the sea ice near the ship.

At every port of call, the *Amundsen* moored out in the bay in deeper waters. A barge was lowered from the ship to ferry participants back and forth. On board, a battery of tests were performed. In addition to health questionnaires, clinical measurements, blood tests, and dietary surveys, we also measured bone density and used ultrasound to detect atherosclerosis in the carotid arteries and the thickness of abdominal fat. Both the current and former premier of the NWT volunteered to be tested. We were warmly welcomed wherever we went. At Cambridge Bay, the community held a feast in honour of the visiting research team.

We were initially concerned about our ship triggering memories of the 1950s and 1960s, when another coast guard ship, the *CD Howe*, conducted chest x-rays of the Inuit people. If they were found to have TB, they would be kept on board and eventually taken to sanatoria in the south. Many were not even allowed to say goodbye to their families on shore and were never heard from again. It is a particularly shameful example of the paternalistic and colonial treatment of Indigenous people by the Canadian state. We were reassured by community leaders that, far from harmful, our visit would be considered an act of reconciliation. Whenever we left a community, the captain would invite to the bridge members of the Inuit staff from that community to toot the horn to bid goodbye to friends and family.

Life on board was never dull—we had games, singalongs, Inuktitut lessons, and, towards the end, an amateur theatrics evening in the tradition of Royal Navy sailors stuck aboard icebound wintering ships. Local people brought on board Inuit country foods and we had a feast, accompanied by explanations on what these foods meant to the people. Yes, there was a bar, open every second evening, with a limit of four drinks per person. The *Amundsen*'s home port was Québec, the majority of the crew was Québécois, and the operating language was French. Crew and survey staff got along famously, and, for one dinner, we dressed up as waiters and waitresses and served the crew.

The North American continental land mass ends at Bellot Strait (two kilometres wide, twenty-five kilometres long). We sailed through the windy strait, a critical corridor in the Northwest Passage. The crew threatened to dunk all first timers to transit this route into the icy ocean as a rite of passage, in full survival gear of course, but somehow forgot to do it.

Conducting research on a ship visiting multiple coastal communities was more efficient than flying crew and equipment into these communities one at a time. It did not come cheap. We were told that the *Amundsen* cost about $50,000 a day to operate, and the sailors were free. We counted 2,525 kilograms of survey-related freight in 260 boxes. There were some forty survey team members—interviewers, interpreters, nurses, lab technicians, dietitians, and one scientist with an ill-defined role.

IPY seemed to have reinvigorated Arctic research in Canada. Arctic warming poses tremendous strategic, political, environmental, and socioeconomic challenges for Canada, especially for the Indigenous people who live there. In 2007, the federal government promulgated a Northern Strategy, which proposed building a state-of-the-art research station in Nunavut to rival those built in Antarctica by other countries. The government commissioned the Canadian Council of Academies to convene an international panel on science priorities for the Canadian Arctic. I was one of only two Canadians on the panel, and probably there as the token public health researcher. We met in Helsinki and produced a report, which basically said that Canada was doing the right things and was on the right track. The government got what it wanted to hear. In 2014, construction for the Canadian High Arctic Research Station commenced in Cambridge Bay, Nunavut. The facility officially opened in 2019, operated by a new agency called Polar Knowledge Canada.

Apart from work-related visits to the circumpolar North, Valerie and I embarked on an Adventure Canada cruise in the summer of 2013. It was a North Atlantic voyage that started in Aberdeen, Scotland, and stopped in the Shetlands, the Faroes, Iceland, and ended in Greenland—the kind of route that the Vikings had likely taken centuries ago. Adventure Canada operated a much smaller ship than the typical cruise ship, but a cozy one. The emphasis was on nature photography, hiking, and birdwatching. There were several experts on board, including an Arctic archeologist, a wildlife photographer, a folk singer, and a man who flew with the geese on an ultralight plane. When we docked in Reykjavik, the social convener organized a soccer match with a team of Icelandic senior citizens. Anyone on board who had once kicked a ball was dragooned onto the ship's team. As expected, the Icelanders, old they might be, were fine specimens of health and vigour. I need not dwell on the outcome of the match.

With a checkmark next to the Faroe Islands, I can now claim that I have travelled to all eight Member States of the Arctic Council, and at least one northern region from each country.

I mentioned earlier that I had led several team grants awarded by CIHR since its inception. Two of these focused specifically on the North, one on chronic disease prevention (2006 to 2011), and the other on health system improvement (2013-18). Both involved intensive partnerships with community organizations and decision-makers in territorial governments and regional health authorities. An important legacy of these team grants was the establishment of health research centres in each of the three territorial capitals, repatriating research to the North. These were founded and nurtured by three dedicated northerners who were passionate about health research: Susan Chatwood in Yellowknife, Gwen Healey Akearok in Iqaluit, and Jody Butler Walker in Whitehorse. With sheer determination and perseverance, and despite constant funding insecurity, they developed the three centres into *bona fide* research institutes. These went beyond the traditional role of facilitating research (i.e. doing all the groundwork for visiting southern academics such as logistics, hiring local staff, and community consultations) to planning, executing and disseminating their own research projects, financed by research grants and contracts that were awarded to them as principal investigators.

U of A considers itself the northernmost research-intensive university in Canada, with a special responsibility for its backyard—the Canadian North. Public health infrastructure and services are woefully underdeveloped in all three northern territories, yet they also offer incredible opportunities for public health training and research. As dean of SPH, I strove to develop this outreach as part of its core mission, given my prior extensive involvement in the North.

In the dead of winter in 2017, I held a retreat for key SPH staff and faculty in Yellowknife, where they met government representatives, visited Indigenous organizations, and held a public meeting to promote our graduate programs, for which there was quite an interest among middle managers and health professionals in the health care system. One would be surprised by the number of Edmontonians who had never ventured into the NWT, despite its proximity. My intention in bringing such a large contingent was to provide context and a buy-in for the northern strategy that the school would develop. A midnight trip to a frozen lake to watch the aurora borealis certainly did the trick in terms of team building.

With newly appointed northern based adjunct professors and elders-in-residence, Yellowknife, 2018

I pushed forward several initiatives in my final two years as dean in order to build a foundation for SPH to become a nationally and internationally recognized centre of excellence in northern health. We signed an affiliation agreement with the Institute for Circumpolar Health Research, led by Susan Chatwood, providing research space and supervision for SPH students and liaising with local governments. We appointed Susan as a full-time faculty member based at both Yellowknife and Edmonton, with a research focus on health system improvement. She was soon awarded U of A's McCalla professorship to develop a northern-focused curriculum that incorporated Indigenous values. We allocated one Canada Research Chair position to northern health, which was awarded to Sherilee Harper, an internationally-recognized expert on the health impact of Arctic climate change. We began active recruitment of graduate students from the NWT. Unique to the university, we appointed northern and Indigenous scholars and leaders as elders-in-residence and adjunct faculty who actively participated in teaching and orienting students to Indigenous values. They were all highly respected and had served their communities over decades, having a wide range of expertise and experience.

One elder-in-residence was Be'sha Blondin, a Sahtu Dene elder who had devoted her life to improving the health of Indigenous people, especially youths. She delivered land-based healing programs and taught ceremonies, healing practices, cultural competency, and traditional knowledge approaches to wellness. The other was Rassi Nashalik, an Inuit elder committed to the promotion and preservation of *Inuit Qaujimajatuqanfit* (traditional knowledge). A highly-respected media personality with CBC North, her award-winning programs celebrated northerners' achievements but also highlighted problems such as youth suicides.

The adjunct professors were:

» François Paulette, a former Dene National Chief who was actively engaged in land claims negotiations and travelled extensively internationally to speak on Indigenous rights, spiritual healing, and environmental protection. He had served as chair of the Elders Council of the Stanton Territorial Hospital in Yellowknife.

» Denise McDonald served in leadership roles in the education and health fields in the NWT, including as education superintendent of the Beaufort Delta Education Council and wellness director of the Gwich'in Tribal Council.

» John B. Zoe, director of Dedat'eetsaa (Tlicho Research and Training Institute) and senior advisor to the Tlicho Government. Dedicated to preserving, reviving, and celebrating the culture and language of the Tlicho people, he helped revitalize traditional activities among youths. He was awarded an honorary doctorate from University of Alberta and appointed a member of the Order of the Northwest Territories.

» Jim Martin had served the Tlicho communities for decades as a teacher, principal, band manager, and education superintendent. As CEO of the Tlicho Community Services Agency, he integrated delivery of health, education, and child and family services into the Tlicho communities. Currently the senior policy advisor to the Tlicho Government, he received an award from the Institute of Public Administration of Canada for innovative management.

» Sharon Firth is an accomplished athlete, community leader, and advocate for youths. A four-time Olympian in cross-country skiing, she received many awards including the Order of Canada, an honorary doctorate from the U of Alberta, and induction into the Canadian Sports Hall of Fame. She has served as Youth Programs Advisor and was instrumental in creating a Youth Secretariat in the Government of the NWT.

The announcement of these appointments in Yellowknife in 2018 brought me back full circle to my first foray into Canada North of 60 in the same city in 1982.

8.

Alpine Sunset

My journeys north have indeed ended. The place Valerie and I chose for our retirement was Fernie, British Columbia, on the edge of the Southern Canadian Rockies, less than eighty kilometres from the United States border. We substituted high latitude for high altitude, as the City of Fernie is nestled beneath Mount Fernie, which is 2,200 metres above sea level. The great outdoors offers cross-country skiing and snowshoeing in the winter, and hiking and kayaking in the summer. Valerie's summers are consumed by gardening, an activity to which she is devoted. And so, we have settled into the next phase of our lives as retired persons . . .

Steven

Robin

At our 40th wedding anniversary dinner, Toronto, 2019

Our home in Fernie, BC

Celebrating the career of
Dean Kue Young

Thursday, June 21 | 4-6 p.m.

South Atrium, 3rd Floor
Edmonton Clinic Health Academy

Please use the south elevators to access the third floor after 5 p.m.

Journey's end, Edmonton, June 2018

Born in Hong Kong, KUE YOUNG came to Canada to attend McGill University, earning a medical degree in 1973. Subsequently, his interest in global health led him to volunteer as a medical consultant with CUSO in Tanzania. Returning to Canada in 1980, he was appointed medical director in Sioux Lookout Zone, Ontario, which led to his lifelong dedication to Indigenous and Northern health in Canada and the circumpolar regions of the world, focusing on emerging chronic diseases such as diabetes. After working as department head at the University of Manitoba, in 2002 he arrived at the University of Toronto and led a program devoted to the training of Indigenous researchers, and in 2013 he was appointed Dean of the School of Public Health at the University of Alberta. Retired, he lives in Fernie, British Columbia.